BE BULLISH

The Luminous Path

BE BULLISH

The Luminous Path

Build Career Clarity

Edward L. Avila

BE BULLISH
BOOKS

Cover Design by: Marwan C. Harb
Author Photo: Kate Zotova of Pacifica Studios
Foreword by: Sharawn Tipton

ISBN: 979-8-9993796-5-8

First Edition: April 2026

10 9 8 7 6 5 4 3 2 1

QUANTITY PURCHASES:

Schools, companies, professional groups, clubs, and
other organizations may qualify for special terms,
when ordering quantities of this title.
For information, email author at edward@bebullish.co.

"Luminous beings are we, not this crude matter."

- YODA (The Empire Strikes Back)

Dedication

In uncertainty you stand—for you, this path was built

Table Of Contents

Foreword

As Chief Human Resources Officer at Greenhouse, former Chief Diversity Officer and as a Black woman who has navigated these systems firsthand, I have spent my career inside the rooms where hiring decisions are made and increasingly inside the systems that power those decisions.

I have seen how talent is evaluated, how potential is interpreted, and how opportunity is allocated. And I can say with confidence that most students and early-career professionals are never taught how this system actually works—especially those who are first in their families to navigate higher education and professional careers.

Hiring is not random. It is structured. It is relational. It is influenced by signals, sponsorship, access, and perception. Those who understand the mechanics advance faster. Those who do not are often left believing the problem is their capability when in reality it is their access.

This gap often disproportionately affects first generation students and professionals, BIPOC students and professionals, community college transfers, immigrants, veterans, women entering male dominated industries, and individuals with non-linear career paths. When you lack insider networks, you are not lacking talent. You are lacking translation.

For many first-generation students, this translation gap is even more pronounced. Without inherited knowledge of how careers are built, how networks are formed, or how opportunities are accessed, they are often navigating systems for the first time—without a roadmap.

That is why Edward Avila's work matters.

Be Bullish The Luminous Path: Build Career Clarity does something rare. It pulls back the curtain. Drawing from three decades of Silicon Valley recruiting, Edward translates what is often hidden into practical, repeatable action. His *Bullish Career Canvas* provides structure in a process that can feel opaque and intimidating. It moves career development from guesswork to strategy.

What stands out most to me is that this is not a book about fitting in. It is a book about positioning yourself with clarity. The frameworks, checklists, and real-world insights do not ask students to shrink or conform. Instead, they equip readers to navigate systems as they are while building confidence in who they already are.

In my career, I have worked at the intersection of talent, equity, and systems change. I believe deeply that expanding access to opportunity requires both institutional accountability and individual empowerment. Tools like this matter because they help level the playing field without requiring permission. They give readers language, structure, and strategy—especially for those who may not have been given early exposure to how these systems work.

If you care about expanding access, strengthening representation, and building sustainable careers, this book belongs in your hands.

My advice is simple. Take these tools seriously. Apply them consistently. Seek sponsors, not just applications. Understand the system so you can move through it with intention.

And above all—be bullish about your future.

Sharawn Tipton
Chief People Officer
Greenhouse

About the Foreword Author

Sharawn Tipton is Chief People Officer at Greenhouse, the leading hiring platform, where she shapes people strategy to accelerate business growth and strengthen the employee experience.

With more than 20 years of experience across public and private companies, Sharawn has championed the people function as a driver of business success. Her expertise spans Total Rewards and IDEA (Inclusion, Diversity, Equity, and Allyship), and she has led global Human Resources teams while fostering inclusive, high-trust cultures.

Previously, she served as Chief People and Culture Officer at LiveRamp and Chief Diversity Officer at Micron Technology, building global people strategies across the U.S., EMEA, and APAC. Earlier in her career, she held HR leadership roles at Flex, Gensler, and Safeway.

Sharawn serves on the Board of Fair Pay Workplace and as a Board Advisor for College Track – Oakland, mentoring first-generation and underrepresented college students. A proud Oakland native, she is a dedicated advocate for equity and community impact.

Message From the Author

In today's job market, hope alone isn't enough—you need clarity, strategy, and a plan you can own.

If you've ever sent out hundreds of applications only to hear silence, walked out of a career fair feeling invisible, or stared at your résumé wondering if it truly reflects who you are—you're not alone. Today's job search is tougher than ever. Job seekers at all levels—students, recent graduates, and even experienced professionals—are frustrated, overwhelmed, and often left feeling isolated.

I've seen this struggle up close for years. Friends, colleagues, and young professionals in my network often reach out to me for guidance. They're not lacking talent or ambition—what they're missing is a clear starting point. Despite the variety of career tools available, I've yet to see one that pulls everything together into a simple, actionable framework. What's needed is a one-page roadmap that helps job seekers plan and test the twelve building blocks of career readiness—something practical that sparks conversations, fuels brainstorming, and guides real decisions.

Over the past 30 years as a Talent Acquisition Executive, I've partnered with countless job seekers and collaborated closely with university career centers. And yet, I've consistently noticed the same gap: there is no common, universal tool that students and professionals can rely on for clarity and direction in their career journey.

That's why I designed the *Bullish Career Canvas*—inspired by Ash Maurya's *Lean Canvas*, a groundbreaking one-page business planning tool used by entrepreneurs worldwide. Just as Lean Canvas gave entrepreneurs a clear, structured way to test and refine their ideas, the *Bullish Career Canvas* gives job seekers a structured way to brainstorm, validate and refine their career readiness.

It's not meant to replace the valuable resources of career centers, mentors, or coaching programs. Instead, it's built to complement them—a living, adaptable framework you can carry into any career conversation.

My hope is simple: that this tool becomes your anchor in the storm. Something practical, empowering, and portable that helps you not only reflect on your career goals but also take bold, confident action in today's competitive job market.

—Edward Avila

Introduction

What is *Be Bullish The Luminous Path: Build Career Clarity?*

Over the years, I've had the privilege of witnessing teamwork at its best while facilitating brainstorming sessions with engineering and product teams. There's something remarkable about a group of smart, driven people gathered around a whiteboard, sticky notes in hand. Ideas surface, assumptions get tested, and suddenly, clarity begins to take shape.

One tool that consistently made these sessions effective was the *Lean Canvas*, a model developed by Ash Maurya and used by many entrepreneurs and startup teams to develop their business strategies. This simple, one-page framework allows you to visualize your ideas, highlight risks, and identify the key elements essential to business success. There's nothing complicated about it—each idea goes on a sticky note, one per color-coded block. The real power of the model lies in its adaptability: ideas can be moved, refined, or replaced as new insights emerge.

What struck me most about this business tool wasn't just the tool's simplicity—it was the energy it created. Teams felt ownership. They could see their thinking come alive on the canvas. And together, they built a clearer, shared picture of their path forward.

Fast forward to my conversations with job seekers—college students, recent graduates, and professionals. Many shared the same struggles: lack of direction, scattered effort, and no real system to measure progress.

That's when it hit me. They needed exactly what entrepreneurs and startup teams already use: a framework to brainstorm, test ideas, and refine direction over time.

If the Lean Canvas could help entrepreneurs make sense of business ideas, why couldn't a similar approach help professionals make sense of their careers? Why not create a simple, one-page framework that allows people to map out their challenges, goals, values, and actions with the same clarity and focus?

That question became the "aha" moment that led to the creation of the *Bullish Career Canvas*.

The *Bullish Career Canvas* is a career operating system organized into four phases:

- AIM – *What you want:* Define the roles or directions you want to pursue.

- FIT – *Where you belong:* Evaluate how your interests, strengths, values, and desired impact align with those roles.

- ACTION – *What you do*: Take deliberate steps that move you toward your target direction.

- EVIDENCE – *How you prove progress:* Collect signals that show whether you are gaining traction—skills developed, projects completed, interviews secured, or feedback received.

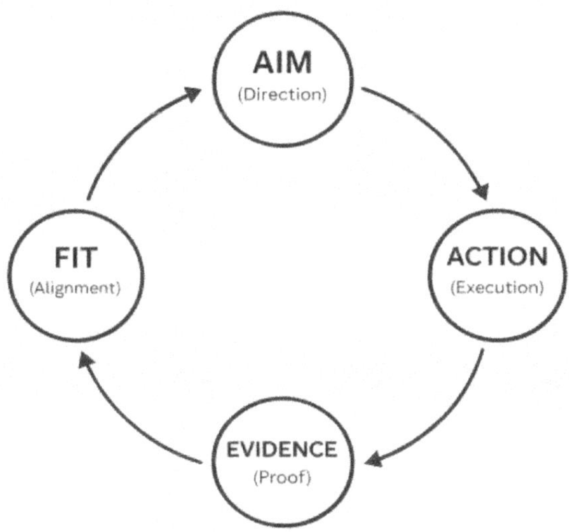

Figure 0.1: Bullish Career Operating System

Together, these four phases transform career exploration from guesswork into a structured process (see **Figure 0.1**).

A Peek at the Bullish Career Canvas in Action

Not long ago, I met Jack, an early-career professional working as a business analyst at a mid-sized tech company. From the outside, things looked stable. He had a solid role, a good team, and a steady paycheck. But when we started talking about his career direction, his answer was simple:

"I'm not stuck… but I'm not sure I'm moving forward either."

Jack had been exploring job opportunities on and off for months. He bookmarked roles, skimmed job descriptions, and occasionally applied. But when it came time to explain what he wanted—or why he was a strong candidate—his answers felt scattered.

That's when I introduced him to the *Bullish Career Canvas*.

We printed the canvas and started with a simple exercise: spend ten minutes filling in each block with whatever came to mind. No overthinking. No perfect answers. Just a first pass.

In the **Challenges** block, Jack wrote:

- "Unclear career direction"
- "Not confident telling my story"

In **Desired Roles**, he listed two paths he had been considering:

- Product Analyst
- Data Analyst

When we moved to **Essential Skills**, something clicked. Many of the roles he was interested in required stronger SQL skills, data visualization experience, and the ability to communicate insights clearly to stakeholders—areas where he had some exposure, but not enough depth.

Then came the **Skill/Experience Gaps** block.

Instead of feeling discouraged, Jack paused.

"For the first time," he said, "I can actually see what I'm missing."

The gaps weren't barriers—they were signals.

In the **Strategic Actions** section, he wrote three immediate steps:

- Enroll in an advanced SQL course
- Build one end-to-end data project for a portfolio
- Reach out to two colleagues working in analytics roles

In **Support Channels**, he identified:

- a former manager
- a colleague in the data team
- an alumni connection from his university

Finally, in the **Success Indicators** block, he defined what progress would look like:

- A completed portfolio project
- Two informational conversations
- Increased confidence explaining his strengths

When Jack stepped back and looked at the page, something shifted.

What once felt like scattered thoughts and uncertainty had become a structured plan.

The answers weren't perfect. Some would change. Others would evolve with time. But for the first time, Jack had clarity—not because he had everything figured out, but because he finally had a system.

That's the power of the *Bullish Career Canvas*. It turns thinking into structure—and structure into progress. It is a career operating system designed to guide your decisions over time.

It doesn't give you all the answers.

But it gives you a system to start asking the right questions—and a way to move forward with intention.

This story about Jack shows how one professional turned uncertainty into direction. On a single page, the *Bullish Career Canvas* organizes twelve interconnected blocks that help you:

- Identify your challenges.

- Define your goals.

- Sharpen your unique value.

- Take measurable, focused steps forward.

I first introduced this tool in my book *Be Bullish 101: Make the Big Leap from College to the Workplace* and continued refining it through many career coaching sessions. The response confirmed what I suspected: professionals at every stage crave a framework that is clear and repeatable.

Many people printed out the *Bullish Career Canvas*—scribbling notes, adding sticky reminders, personalizing it until it reflected their own story. No two canvases looked the same.

And that's the point. It's not a static worksheet—it's a living system designed to evolve as you do.

The *Bullish Career Canvas* helps turn uncertainty into clarity, frustration into focus, and static goals into action. It's a luminous path that shines a light on where you are, where you're going, and what steps to take next.

That's why this book exists—to give the *Bullish Career Canvas* the spotlight it deserves and to help you design a career strategy grounded in clarity, evidence, and intentional progress. Because in the end, your career is more than a series of jobs or titles—it reflects your growth, your values, and the impact you choose to make.

As Yoda reminds us in *The Empire Strikes Back*:

"Luminous beings are we, not this crude matter."

Your career is not defined by a single line on your résumé. It is defined by the clarity you build—and the system you choose to follow.

How To Use This Book

This is not another career advice book—it's a system you will use. This book is meant to be a living document—a guide you can return to whether you're focused on your current situation or planning your next steps. It's not static, and it's not about perfection. The *Bullish Career Canvas* is designed to help you iterate, refine, and gain clarity over time.

That system is the *Bullish Career Canvas*—a one-page framework made up of 12 interconnected blocks that bring structure, clarity, and direction to your career decisions (see **Figure 0.2**).

CHALLENGES What's blocking my progress right now?	DESIRED ROLE(S) What job roles or functions am I aiming for?	TARGETED COMPANIES + SECTORS What industries or employers am I focusing on?	SKILL/EXPERIENCE GAPS What am I missing today?	STRATEGIC ACTIONS What steps will I take now?
	UNIQUE VALUE PROPOSITION + THE PITCH What's my personal "wow" factor?	ESSENTIAL SKILLS + CAREER VALUES What skills (hard & soft) are required for these roles?	AVAILABLE RESOURCES What resources can I leverage to advance my career?	SUPPORT CHANNELS Who can offer me guidance and support?
SUCCESS INDICATORS What does success look like?		KEY METRICS How will I measure my progress?	CONTINUOUS LEARNING How will I keep expanding my knowledge and skills?	

Figure 0.2: Bullish Career Canvas

The book is organized into four core parts, each covering a section of the *Bullish Career Canvas*. In total, there are 12 blocks, divided into these four groups of three. Each chapter highlights one block, explains its purpose, presents a helpful framework, and shows completed examples—so you can see how the career canvas applies at different stages of the career journey.

To make the canvas easier to use, the 12 blocks are grouped into four: AIM, FIT, ACTION, and EVIDENCE (see **Figure 0.3**).

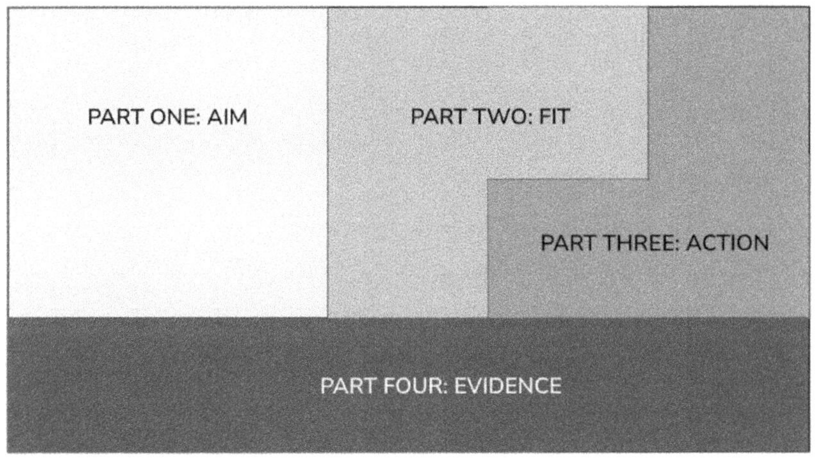

Figure 0.3: Four Core Parts to Bullish Career Canvas

The canvas operates in a continuous cycle: AIM → FIT → ACTION → EVIDENCE.

These parts are not steps you complete once—they form a loop you return to as your career evolves, helping you refine your direction, test your assumptions, and build momentum over time.

At the end of each part, you'll find gating criteria—a quick self-check to confirm you're ready to move forward.

Part I — AIM

1) Challenge(s) · 2) Desired Role(s) · 3) Unique Value Proposition + Pitch

- Define your blockers, clarify your target roles, and shape your pitch.
- Gating criteria: You can state your top two blockers, list 1–3 roles and deliver a 30-second pitch.

Part II — FIT

4) Targeted Companies/Sectors · 5) Essential Skills + Career Values · 6) Skill/Experience Gaps

- Align industries with your skills and values and spotlight the gaps to close.
- Gating criteria: You have a short list of 10–20 target companies, a skills/values map, and a prioritized gap list.

Part III — ACTION

7) Available Resources 8) Strategic Actions · 9) Support Channels

- Convert insights into weekly actions and enlist resources and people to help.
- Gating criteria: You've scheduled a 2–4 weeks action plan, identified resources, and secured at least two support partners.

Part IV — EVIDENCE

10) Success Indicators · 11) Key Metrics · 12) Continuous Learning

- Define what success looks like, measure progress, and build a learning cadence.

- Gating criteria: You've set outcome goals, chosen weekly metrics, and committed to one learning plan with dates.

How to Work with This Book

- Start with Part I. Don't skip ahead—the canvas builds on itself. Complete the gating criteria before moving forward.

- Print or duplicate the canvas. Keep a master version and update it monthly.

- Draft fast. Each block should take 15–20 minutes on your first pass. First answers don't need to be perfect—they just need to be written.

- Experiment weekly. Every career plan starts with a hypothesis—treat actions like tests: try, measure, learn, and adapt.

- Share your canvas. Show it to mentors, advisors, or peers for feedback and accountability.

- Measure 3–5 key metrics. Applications, interviews, outreach, or portfolio updates—choose what matters now and review weekly. What gets measured improves.

- Iterate monthly. Revisit your canvas, update what's changed, and archive old versions. Progress is visible when you compare past to present.

- Lean into your stage. Students may lean on resources, grads on companies, seasoned pros on value propositions. The same canvas flexes across all stages.

- Stay human. Your UVP and pitch aren't slogans—they're your authentic story.

- Be bullish. Don't wait for perfect conditions. Act, learn, and refine. That's how focus becomes readiness.

Why Sticky Notes Matter

In this book, you'll notice we end each chapter with a sticky note. That's not an accident. Sticky notes are simple, low-tech, and accessible to everyone — but in design thinking and innovation, they've long been prized because they capture ideas, can be rearranged, and reveal how the parts connect to the whole.

In the *Bullish Career Canvas*, each sticky note is more than a quote—it's a design material for your career. By writing them down, you're not just collecting reminders; you're shaping your luminous path, one piece at a time. Step back at the end, and you'll see how each note—each action, reflection, or commitment—comes together as your complete career clarity system.

Think of this book as your career whiteboard: messy at first, clearer with every pass. Each iteration sharpens your vision, strengthens your confidence, and moves you closer to the future you want to pursue.

And remember—you don't have to do this alone. The career canvas can be a powerful tool to bring into a conversation with your career center counselor, mentor, or trusted advisor. Sharing your career canvas gives others a clear window into your goals, challenges, and progress, making their guidance sharper, more relevant, and more actionable.

PART ONE

AIM

1

CHAPTER

BULLISH CAREER CANVAS

Before you make progress in your career, you need direction. That's what the *Bullish Career Canvas* gives you: a one-page roadmap made up of 12 interconnected blocks, grouped into four parts—Aim, Fit, Action, and Evidence (see **Figure 1.1**). These parts don't replace the canvas—they organize it.

Each block asks you a simple, personal question. But behind each question are deeper prompts designed to help you reflect honestly, take ownership, and identify your next steps. You don't need to have perfect answers right now—you need a starting point and this book will guide you block by block.

By the time you reach the end, you'll have a clear career readiness roadmap that's yours to own, refine, and share with mentors, advisors, or career counselors.

Clarity is not about having every answer. It's about knowing what you are solving for—and why it matters.

Most professionals move before they analyze. They apply before they understand the requirements. They react before they assess alignment. Clarity requires the opposite sequence: understand first, move second. Without that pause, effort becomes motion without direction.

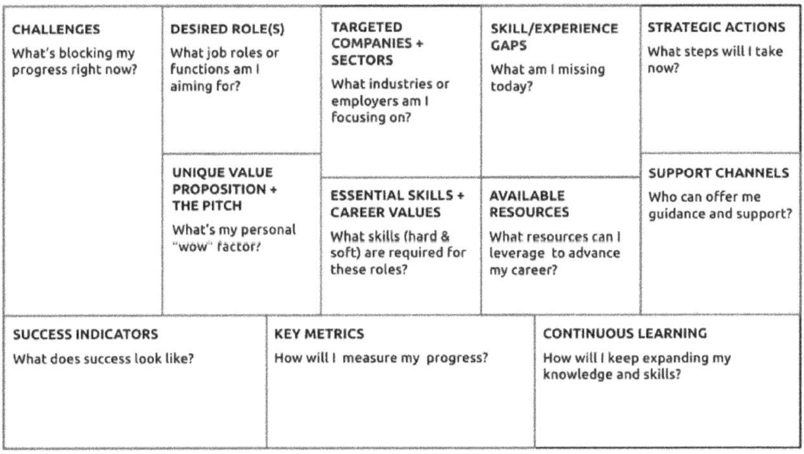

CHALLENGES What's blocking my progress right now?	DESIRED ROLE(S) What job roles or functions am I aiming for?	TARGETED COMPANIES + SECTORS What industries or employers am I focusing on?	SKILL/EXPERIENCE GAPS What am I missing today?	STRATEGIC ACTIONS What steps will I take now?
	UNIQUE VALUE PROPOSITION + THE PITCH What's my personal "wow" factor?	ESSENTIAL SKILLS + CAREER VALUES What skills (hard & soft) are required for these roles?	AVAILABLE RESOURCES What resources can I leverage to advance my career?	SUPPORT CHANNELS Who can offer me guidance and support?
SUCCESS INDICATORS What does success look like?	KEY METRICS How will I measure my progress?		CONTINUOUS LEARNING How will I keep expanding my knowledge and skills?	

Figure 1.1: Bullish Career Canvas

The Four Parts of the Canvas

Part I — AIM

Where are you now, and where do you want to go?

1. Challenges — What's blocking my progress right now?

- Are your blockers mostly internal (confidence, clarity, mindset) or external (skills, opportunities, connections)?

- Which challenges can you control or influence, and which are outside your control?

- Which challenge causes you the most frustration or stalls you the most?

- If you solved one blocker this month, which would make the biggest difference?

2. Desired Role(s) — What job roles or functions are you aiming for?

- Which job titles, industries, or functions excite you most right now?

- Are you aiming for one role, or exploring two or three possible paths?

- Why these roles—what about them feels like a fit with your strengths or interests?

- If you had to explain you target role to someone in one sentence, could you?

3. Unique Value Proposition + Pitch — What's my personal "wow" factor?

- What do you do better or differently than most people at your level?

- Which skills, experiences, or traits do others often compliment you on?

- How would you describe your story and motivation in two to three sentences?

- Can you communicate your pitch out loud in 30 seconds with confidence?

Part II — FIT

Do your goals align with industries, companies, and skills?

4. Targeted Companies/Sectors — What industries or employers are you focusing on?

- Which industries or sectors feel most aligned with your goals?

- Which 10–20 companies would you be most excited to work for?

- Do your current skills and experiences match what these companies need?

- Have you researched whether these companies are growing, hiring, or stable?

5. Essential Skills + Career Values — What skills (hard & soft) are required for these roles? What values matter for you to thrive?

- What are the technical or hard skills required to succeed in your target role?

- What are the soft skills (communication, leadership, adaptability) that matter?

- What personal values do you need in a workplace to feel engaged and supported?

- Which of my values are non-negotiable (e.g., growth, flexibility, collaboration)?

6. Skill/Experience Gaps — What are you missing today?

- Which required skills or experiences do you not yet have?
- Which of these gaps could you realistically close in the next 6–12 months?
- How do your gaps compare to what peers or competitors for these roles have?
- Which gaps could you reframe as learning opportunities during interviews?

Part III — ACTION

How will you move forward with intention?

7. Available Resources — What resources can you leverage to advance your career?

- What services at your school, workplace, or community, are you underusing?
- Which professors, advisors, or industry professionals could you reach out to?
- Are there online platforms, courses, or groups that could accelerate your growth?
- What free or low-cost resources are you overlooking?

8. Strategic Actions — What steps will you take now?

- What 3–5 actions will you commit to in the next 30 days?

- Are you spreading yourself too thin, or focusing on the most impactful steps?
- Which actions will move you closer to interviews or opportunities fastest?
- What will you stop doing to create space for better actions?

9. Support Channels — Who can offer you guidance and support?

- Who in your network can give you advice, feedback, or referrals?
- Are there alumni, peers, or mentors that you can reach out to this month?
- Do you have at least two accountability partners to keep you on track?
- Are you asking for specific help, or just waiting for support to show up?

Part IV — EVIDENCE

How will you measure progress and stay ready?

10. Success Indicators — What does success look like for you?

- How will you know that you're moving in the right direction?
- Is success about milestones (internship, full-time role, promotion) or learning?
- What small wins will you celebrate along the way?

- What would "career readiness" mean to you one year from now?

11. Key Metrics — How will you measure your progress?

- Which 3–5 numbers matter most (applications, interviews, outreach)?

- Are you tracking your activity weekly to spot patterns and results?

- Do your metrics reflect effort (inputs) or outcomes (results)—or both?

- Are you holding yourself accountable with data, not just feelings?

12. Continuous Learning — How will you keep expanding your knowledge and skills?

- Which skills do you need to develop to stay competitive in your field?

- How often will you commit to learning (monthly, quarterly, yearly)?

- Will you use courses, certifications, books, or on-the-job projects to grow?

- How will you measure and showcase your learning over time?

Your Career, On One Page

The *Bullish Career Canvas* puts all of these blocks in one place. On a single sheet, you can map your challenges, define your goals, align them with companies and skills, turn them into actions, and measure my results.

This isn't just a worksheet—it's your strategic whiteboard. Messy at first, clearer with each pass. With every iteration, my vision sharpens, my confidence grows, and my next steps become easier to see.

Quick Start Exercise

Before going deeper, do a **fast first pass** on the canvas:

- Spend **10 minutes** sketching answers in each block.

- Keep it messy—short words or phrases are enough. Use sticky notes—they provide flexibility, easy updates, and seamless collaboration.

- Don't overthink it. This not about getting it right. It's about getting it written.

By the time you finish this book, this canvas will look completely different—and that's the point. You don't complete this canvas once—you return to it as your career evolves.

Transition to Challenges

Every journey toward clarity begins with obstacles. Before you set your sights on roles or pitches, you need to name what's holding you back. Let's begin with your challenges—the barriers that, once identified, become your stepping stones forward.

2

CHAPTER

CHALLENGES

Every career journey begins with obstacles. Some are visible—like not having enough experience for the roles you want. Others are quieter: self-doubt, unclear direction, or not knowing how to articulate your story. But here's the reality: you can't solve what you haven't named.

When job seekers reach out to me, it's often at a breaking point. They're sending résumés into the void, getting rejection emails, or sitting through interviews that go nowhere. Frustration builds until it feels like the system is stacked against them.

Sometimes that breaking point is subtle. It's the quiet moment after another rejection email. It's watching a classmate announce a new internship while you refresh your inbox. It's the growing fear that maybe you're the only one who hasn't figured it out yet. Those moments sting more than people admit.

If the job market feels heavier than it used to, you're not imagining it. Over the past year alone, more than a thousand companies have announced mass layoffs across industries—from tech to healthcare to finance. Experts are now using a term that didn't exist a few years ago: *layoff fatigue*. It describes not only the exhaustion of those who were let go, but also the anxiety of those still employed, waiting for the next round. When uncertainty becomes constant, even high performers begin to question their footing. Uncertainty distorts perception; what once felt like momentum can suddenly feel like fragility.

If this sounds familiar, pause for a second. Take a breath. Your frustration isn't a sign you're failing—it's a signal. The first step toward momentum is naming what's really blocking you. Once you put words to the problem, you can stop spinning and start strategizing.

Most people skip this step. They react to rejection by sending more applications. They interpret silence as failure rather than feedback. Motion replaces analysis. But clarity begins with diagnosis, and diagnosis requires honesty. Without clarity, even talented people default to reaction instead of strategy. That is why naming your challenges is not optional—it is stabilizing.

This process can be uncomfortable. It requires looking at your situation without defensiveness and without self-judgment. It means asking, *"What's actually happening?"* instead of, *"Why is this happening to me?"* That shift alone changes everything.

Why This Block Matters

If you skip this step and rush straight into applications, you risk three things:

- **Wasted effort.** Applying to dozens of jobs that don't fit.

- **Low confidence.** Comparing yourself to others without recognizing your strengths.

- **Scattered direction.** Saying yes to opportunities that pull you off course.

Challenges come in two forms:

- **Internal challenges**: mindset, confidence, fear of rejection, unclear goals.

- **External challenges**: lack of experience, no professional network, limited opportunities.

Both are valid. Both must be acknowledged. Ignoring one side creates blind spots. And blind spots stall progress. Unexamined challenges create reactive behavior. Examined challenges create strategy.

Many people prefer to blame the market because it feels safer. *"The economy is bad." "Hiring is slow." "There aren't enough opportunities."* Sometimes that's true in some industries. But even in difficult markets, some people gain traction. The difference is rarely luck alone. It's clarity about what can be influenced and what cannot.

Naming your challenges isn't weakness—it's strategy. Once you see them clearly, you can design a plan to move through them deliberately. That's why this is Block 1 of the *Bullish Career Canvas* (see **Figure 2.1**).

CHALLENGES What's blocking my progress right now?	DESIRED ROLE(S) What job roles or functions am I aiming for?	TARGETED COMPANIES + SECTORS What industries or employers am I focusing on?	SKILL/EXPERIENCE GAPS What am I missing today?	STRATEGIC ACTIONS What steps will I take now?
	UNIQUE VALUE PROPOSITION + THE PITCH What's my personal "wow" factor?	ESSENTIAL SKILLS + CAREER VALUES What skills (hard & soft) are required for these roles?	AVAILABLE RESOURCES What resources can I leverage to advance my career?	SUPPORT CHANNELS Who can offer me guidance and support?
SUCCESS INDICATORS What does success look like?	KEY METRICS How will I measure my progress?	CONTINUOUS LEARNING How will I keep expanding my knowledge and skills?		

Figure 2.1: Block 1—Challenges

Challenges: What's blocking my progress right now?

Guiding Questions

Before you begin, ask yourself:

- Are my biggest challenges internal or external?
- Which challenge keeps you stuck the most?
- Which blockers are within your control to address right now?
- If you solved just one challenge this month, which would create the biggest lift?

These questions narrow your focus and reduce overwhelm.

Overwhelm often comes not from having too many problems, but from not knowing where to start. Once you isolate one or two pressure points, the fog begins to lift.

How to Work with This Block

Step 1: Brain Dump

Set a timer for 10 minutes and write down everything you believe is blocking your progress. No editing, no judgment.

Examples might include:

- "I don't know what role I want."
- "I've applied to 100 jobs with no responses."
- "Networking feels intimidating."
- "I don't have internship experience."

Notice the language you use. Are your statements fixed ("I'm not good enough") or transitional ("I haven't developed this yet")? The difference matters.

Fixed language freezes progress. Transitional language invites growth. The words you choose quietly shape what you believe is possible.

Step 2: Sort Them

Once your list is complete, divide it into two groups:

- **Internal blockers** (confidence, clarity, fear, motivation).
- **External blockers** (skills, connections, résumé gaps, opportunities).

This separation helps you see what's in your control versus what may require new strategies or outside help. Clarity increases when responsibility becomes visible.

When responsibility becomes visible, so does power. You may not control everything, but you almost always control something.

Map Them Using the Challenge Matrix

Sorting is a good start, but not all challenges are equal. Some you can control, others you cannot. To get clarity, use the Challenge Matrix shown in **Figure 2.2.**

	Internal	**External**
In Your Control	Things you can influence through mindset shifts, habits, or preparation. *Examples:* reframing rejection, practicing interview answers, setting routines.	Things you can improve with effort and resources. *Examples:* learning a new skill, updating my résumé, attending networking events.
Out of Your Control	Internal factors you can notice but not fully eliminate. *Examples:* natural nerves before interviews, perfectionism tendencies.	External factors you can't control but must adapt around. *Examples:* job market downturns, company hiring freezes, geographic limitations.

Figure 2.2: The Challenge Matrix

How to use it:

1. Take your challenge list.
2. Place each challenge into one of the four quadrants.
3. Focus your energy on the top row (challenges *in your control*).
4. Acknowledge, but don't obsess over, the bottom row.

The goal is not to eliminate every obstacle. It is to concentrate your efforts where leverage exists.

Energy misdirected is exhausting. Energy focused is empowering.

Step 3 — Prioritize Top Two

Circle the two challenges that feel most urgent. These are your starting points. Focusing on everything at once is overwhelming. Focusing on two creates momentum.

Momentum builds confidence. Confidence builds clarity. And clarity reduces the emotional weight that uncertainty carriers.

Step 4 — Reframe as Questions

Then turn each challenge into an action-oriented question.

Example:

- From: *"I don't know what role I want."*
- To: *"What steps can I take to clarify the types of roles that fit my skills and interests?"*

Reframing a challenge as a question moves you from emotion to intention. The moment you convert a complaint into a question, you shift from feeling stuck to designing your next move.

Emily on the Challenge Matrix

Emily was a sophomore majoring in Communications. When I first met her, she was overwhelmed and didn't know where to start with her job search. Her friends were landing internships, but she felt behind and unsure of herself.

What she didn't say at first was that she felt embarrassed. Embarrassed that she didn't have a plan. Embarrassed that others seemed more certain. That quiet comparison was draining her energy before she began.

When we started working together, Emily's initial list of challenges looked like this:

- "I don't know what I want to do."
- "I've never had an internship."
- "I don't have connections in any industry."
- "I don't know how to talk about myself and what I want after graduation."
- "I feel like I'm not good enough compared to my classmates."

We mapped her challenges onto the Challenge Matrix:

- **Internal / In My Control:** lack of clarity → she could explore career paths with her advisor.

- **Internal / Out of My Control:** nerves before networking events → something she could manage, not eliminate.

- **External / In My Control:** no internship experience → she could apply for campus roles or part-time work.

- **External / Out of My Control:** limited industry connections as a sophomore → would grow naturally over time.

These steps helped Emily her energy. Instead of worrying about what she couldn't control, Emily focused on what she could. She reframed her top two challenges into questions:

- *"What steps can I take to explore possible roles within communications?"*

- *"What's the simplest way to gain relevant experience before junior year?"*

With those questions, Emily set up a meeting with her career center advisor, joined the PR student club, and applied for a part-time social media assistant role on campus. Within a few months, she had both direction and experience.

The lesson: clarity begins by separating what you can control from what you can't.

The turning point wasn't her résumé—it was mapping her challenges as a starting point, choosing what she could control, and reframing them into action. Clarity preceded opportunity.

She didn't solve everything but once she saw movement—even small progress—her confidence began to rebuild.

Exercises for you:

Now it's your turn.

1. **Brain Dump:** Write down every challenge that comes to mind. Don't filter or edit.

2. **Sort:** Label each as internal or external.

3. **Prioritize:** Circle your top two challenges.

4. **Reframe:** Turn each into a question beginning with *"What steps can I take…?"*

5. **Action Step:** Share your top two challenges with a mentor, advisor, or career counselor. Ask: *"Based on these, what's one action you recommend I try this week?"*

Closing Reflection

Your challenges aren't walls; they're signals. By naming them, you've gained visibility. By reframing them, you've built momentum. And momentum, sustained over time, compounds into confidence.

Confidence does not arrive fully formed. It grows from evidence—small actions taken, small wins earned, and small adjustments made.

Tonight, write your top two challenges on sticky notes and place them where you can see them daily—not as reminders of limitation, but as prompts for movement.

Write this on a sticky note:

Place it where you'll see it when doubt creeps in—as a reminder that obstacles point you toward growth.

The CEO-Mindset

- **Challenges are data, not defects.** CEOs face setbacks every quarter—but they measure them to improve. Treat your blockers the same way.

- **Focus where you have leverage.** Don't waste energy on what's out of your control. Invest in the challenges you can influence today.

- **Reframe into strategy.** CEOs don't say, "We have a problem." They ask, "What's our next move?" Apply the same mindset.

- **Build momentum through small wins.** Solving two challenges well creates more progress than juggling ten at once.

Strategic leaders do not avoid friction. They interpret it.

Transition to Desired Role(s)

Now that you've identified your blockers, the next question is: *"Where do you want to go?"*

Challenges illuminate where you stand today. Now it's time to define where you're going. In the next chapter, you'll define your desired roles, so your energy moves with purpose, not scatter.

3

CHAPTER

—————

DESIRED ROLES

Clarity is power. Once you've named your challenges, the next step is deciding where you want to go. Without a defined target role, your energy scatters—you apply broadly, say yes to reactively, and struggle to articulate a coherent story in interviews. When direction is vague, effort becomes exhausting. You can be busy every day and still feel like you're standing still.

Whether you're a graduate, unemployed, or looking for something new, the best job search strategy is to create a plan before you start looking and applying for jobs. Having a plan from the start can make the job search process less intimidating and help you stay organized. More importantly, a plan restores confidence. It replaces the feeling of "hoping something works out" with the discipline of "I know what I'm aiming for."

At this stage, it helps to think about career direction in a slightly different way. Instead of assuming you must immediately choose the perfect role, treat your target role as a *Career Hypothesis.*

A Career Hypothesis is a simple statement of belief about where your skills, interests, and opportunities may intersect. It is not a final decision—it is a starting point for exploration.

For example:

"I believe my analytical skills and interest in business strategy could translate into a role as a business analyst."

Or:

"I believe my experience working with customers and solving problems could translate well into a customer success role."

The purpose of this hypothesis is not to guarantee certainty. It gives you a direction to test. The remaining blocks of the *Bullish Career Canvas* will help you examine whether your hypothesis holds up—by exploring the skills required, identifying gaps, gathering feedback, and building evidence that you can succeed in that role.

By framing your desired role as a hypothesis, you remove the pressure of needing to have everything figured out today. Instead, you begin a structured process of discovery.

Why This Block Matters

When you define the roles or functions, you're aiming for, you give yourself a compass. It doesn't mean you're locked in forever—it means you have direction for the season you're in. A clear target makes every résumé line, LinkedIn update, and networking conversation sharper.

Employers hire for alignment, not ambition. The clearer your direction, the easier it is for others to see where you fit. And when others can see your fit, you begin to see it more clearly yourself. Confidence compounds when alignment becomes visible.

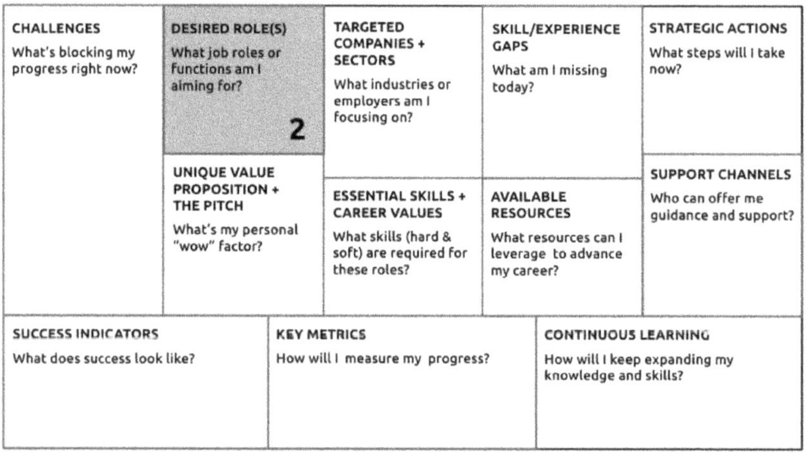

CHALLENGES	DESIRED ROLE(S)	TARGETED COMPANIES + SECTORS	SKILL/EXPERIENCE GAPS	STRATEGIC ACTIONS
What's blocking my progress right now?	What job roles or functions am I aiming for? **2**	What industries or employers am I focusing on?	What am I missing today?	What steps will I take now?
	UNIQUE VALUE PROPOSITION + THE PITCH	ESSENTIAL SKILLS + CAREER VALUES	AVAILABLE RESOURCES	SUPPORT CHANNELS
	What's my personal "wow" factor?	What skills (hard & soft) are required for these roles?	What resources can I leverage to advance my career?	Who can offer me guidance and support?
SUCCESS INDICATORS		KEY METRICS		CONTINUOUS LEARNING
What does success look like?		How will I measure my progress?		How will I keep expanding my knowledge and skills?

Figure 3.1: Block 2—Desired Role(s)

This is why *Desired Role(s)* sits at the core of **Part I — Aim** on the *Bullish Career Canvas* (see **Figure 3.1**). Without direction, challenges remain foggy. With direction, they begin to take shape—and you gain momentum. Direction precedes distinction. When you know where you're going, rejection stings less and feedback becomes useful. The fog begins to lift.

But identifying a desired role isn't about pulling a job title out of thin air. It's about peeling back the layers of who you are and what motivates you. That's where the *Bullish Onion Model* comes in (see **Figure 3.2**).

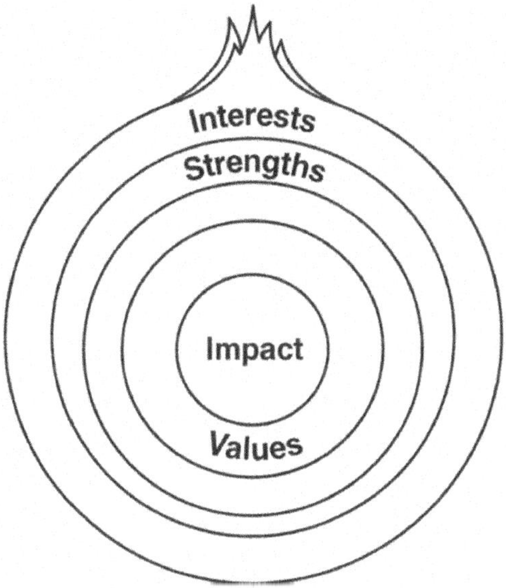

Figure 3.2: Bullish Onion Model

The Bullish Onion Model

To uncover your target roles, you'll move inward, one layer at a time. Ask yourself:

1. **Interests**: What sparks your curiosity? What do you enjoy learning or talking about?

2. **Strengths**: What are you naturally good at or have developed skills in?

3. **Values**: What kind of work environment and impact do you need to thrive?

4. **Impact**: How do you want to contribute to the bigger picture?

Many job seekers choose titles based on familiarity or prestige. But strong career direction rarely comes from guessing. It usually emerges when your values, interests, capabilities, and market opportunities begin to align.

This is where a Career Hypothesis begins to take shape.

A Career Hypothesis is a working assumption about the type of role where your strengths, interests, values, and desired impact may intersect. It is not a final answer—it is a direction worth testing.

The Onion Model forces a deeper question: does the role align with how you think, what you value, and how you want to contribute? A job title might impress others, but alignment sustains you. Misalignment drains you quietly over time.

Each layer sharpens the picture. When all four align, you're not just choosing a job—you're selecting a direction that is sustainable. Sustainability is what separates a short-term win from a long-term trajectory.

And here's the best part: you don't have to do this alone. You can work through the layers on your own for honest self-reflection, or you can collaborate with someone who knows you well—a mentor, a career counselor, even a close friend. Sometimes, an outside perspective can reveal patterns or strengths you've overlooked. Often, others can see your signal before you can.

Guiding Questions

Ask yourself:

- Which job titles, industries, or functions excite you most right now?
- Are you aiming for one role, or exploring two or three possible paths?
- Why these roles—what about them feels like a fit with your strengths or interests?
- If you had to explain your target role to someone in one sentence, could you?

How to Work with This Block

Step 1 — List Possible Roles

Start broad intentionally. Write down any roles, titles, or industries you've thought about—even if they feel out of reach.

Step 2 — Peel Back the Onion

For each role, ask yourself:

- Does it align with your interests?
- Does it use your strengths?
- Does it support your values?
- Does it create the impact you want?

Step 3 — Test for Clarity

Narrow your list. Aim for 1–3 roles that you can articulate in one sentence each. More than three usually signals exploration. Fewer than one signals avoidance.

Step 4 — Validate

Share your target roles with a mentor, advisor, or career counselor. Ask: "Do these roles align with what you see in me?"

Finding Focus

When Richard graduated with an Economics degree, his career path felt wide open. He knew he wanted "something in business," but lacked clarity. That phrase, "something in business", is where many careers stall. It sounds ambitious, but it offers no direction.

When Richard came to me for career coaching, I saw the confusion firsthand. He had submitted dozens of applications for jobs ranging from analyst to HR, but all the effort had yielded only a handful of interviews. He wasn't lazy. He wasn't unqualified. He was simply unfocused.

As we worked through the *Bullish Onion Model*, the layers began to peel back, revealing his core motivations and purpose.

- *Interests:* Richard loved problem-solving and data. He got excited about projects involving numbers.

- *Strengths:* He was strong in Excel, research, and communication. Professors praised his ability to turn data into stories.

- *Values:* Richard wanted growth opportunities and a collaborative team environment.

- *Impact:* He wanted to help businesses make smarter decisions with data.

The model pointed him toward *Business/Data Analyst* roles. Suddenly, his résumé became sharper—every bullet framed around analysis, reporting, and insights. His LinkedIn headline changed to "Aspiring Business Analyst," and his networking conversations gained purpose. Instead of asking, "Are you hiring?" he began asking, "How do you break into analytics?" The tone shifted. The conversations deepened.

The lesson: focus doesn't come from broad intent—it comes from defined direction.

Within six weeks, Richard landed interviews at three companies and accepted an offer as a junior analyst.

Clarity changed his outcomes. But more importantly, it changed his posture. He stopped chasing everything—started pursuing something.

The story of Richard is universal. No matter where you are in your career, the process of finding clarity remains the same.

If you are a student, internships are your laboratory for professional discovery. Experiment with different roles and environments, testing each experience against the layers of your *Onion Model.* Try a marketing internship, shadow an analyst, or take on a student leadership role. Each experience adds valuable data to your career experiment. Data reduces guessing. Patterns reveal direction. Experience replaces anxiety with evidence.

If you have already been in the workforce for a few years, the key is to refine your path, not necessarily to start over. Look back at your past roles and ask yourself: where have you felt most engaged, and which roles drained your energy? Use the *Onion Model* to re-assess your trajectory. Your goal isn't to start over; it's to align your next step more closely with your strengths, values, and desired impact. Refinement is often more powerful than reinvention. Small directional shifts often create bigger long-term returns than dramatic resets.

Exercises for You

1. Role Brainstorm: List every job title that comes to mind.

2. Onion Test: For each, check against Interests, Strengths, Values, Impact.

3. Narrow Down: Circle your top 1–3 roles.

4. One-Liner Pitch: Write one sentence for each role: "I'm aiming for [role] because it fits my [strengths/values]."

5. Validation Step: Share your top roles with a mentor, advisor, or peer for feedback.

Closing Reflection

Your desired roles are your compass, not a prison. They guide your actions today while leaving room for growth tomorrow. Direction creates freedom, not confinement.

Document your top role(s) on a sticky note and keep them visible. Direction, when visible, influences behavior. Let it remind you: every résumé edits, every LinkedIn update, and every conversation can now move in the same direction. Scatter fades when intention is written down.

Write this on a sticky note:

Keep it near your calendar as a reminder that every application is a step toward reaching your luminous future.

The CEO-Mindset

- **Roles are your compass.** CEOs don't chase every opportunity—they choose a direction. Define yours so your actions have focus. Strategy without focus is just activity.

- **Peel back the layers.** Like a market analysis, clarity comes from digging into data. For you, that "data" is your interests, strengths, values, and impact. Clarity is rarely accidental. It's constructed.

- **Keep options strategic.** One to three roles create focus. More than that creates scatter.

- **Validate with advisors.** CEOs test strategy with their board. You should test your direction with mentors and peers.

Transition to the CEO of You, Inc.

You've defined your destination. But direction alone won't differentiate you. To be remembered, you need to sharpen what makes you different.

In Chapter 4, you'll step into the role of the **CEO of You, Inc.**—learning how to manage your career with intention and build distinction through your value proposition.

4

CHAPTER

———

CEO of YOU, INC

It is one of the most powerful and sought-after titles in business. A CEO sets strategy, allocates resources, shapes culture, and carries accountability for results. They are scrutinized by boards, investors, employees, and customers alike. Every move is watched. Every decision carries weight.

Now imagine applying that same level of clarity, accountability, and ownership to your career.

That's the discipline behind the *CEO of You, Inc.*

You may not have a corner office, an executive assistant, or shareholders waiting for quarterly reports. But in a very real way, you are the CEO of your career. Think of your career as your company. Companies that drift lose market position. Careers that drift lose momentum. You are responsible for setting its strategy, managing its growth, building its brand, and ensuring its long-term health.

If you don't assume that role intentionally, someone else will. An employer may define your trajectory. A manager may shape your development by default. Market conditions may dictate your options. In today's climate, many professionals are operating defensively rather than strategically. Some are stacking side hustles as a form of "career insurance." Others are bracing for layoffs that may or may not come. The atmosphere of uncertainty has created a workforce that is busy, cautious, and often exhausted.

But busyness is not strategy. More activity does not automatically produce more security. When fear drives decisions, effort multiplies but clarity diminishes. The result is motion without direction, productivity without positioning.

The CEO mindset offers something different. It shifts you from reactive to proactive. It builds leverage before urgency forces it. It asks not, *"How do I survive this season?"* but *"How do I position myself for strength in the next one?"*

Thinking and acting like a CEO places you back in command. Ownership clarifies trade-offs. Clarity sharpens priorities. And sharpened priorities improve outcomes.

The question is not whether you have the title. The question is whether you are willing to assume the responsibility. You are not just managing your career—you are operating it.

Why This Block Matters

Up until now, this book has helped you define challenges and clarify desired roles. Those are foundational steps. Without a CEO mindset, they risk remaining conceptual—ideas without execution.

CEOs don't have the luxury of drifting, and neither should you.

This chapter equips you with a simple framework for running your career like a high-performing company. It isn't about ego—it's about stewardship.

Six Elements of a CEO Mindset

Here's how the CEO mindset breaks down into six practical elements you can apply right now (see **Figure 4.1**). These six elements functional like a board agenda. Review them regularly. Adjust deliberately:

Figure 4.1: CEO of You, Inc.

1. Personal Operating System

CEOs manage their time, energy, and routines with discipline. For you, that means setting boundaries, creating rituals that boost focus, and avoiding burnout. Time is your scarcest resource—treat it like capital. Executives design their calendar. They do not inherit it.

2. Career Strategy

A CEO sets vision and strategy. You do the same by defining what success means in this season of your career. What roles, industries, and skills are worth investing in? Where will you allocate your effort for the highest long-term return?

3. Network Alignment

Great CEOs align stakeholders. For you, stakeholders are mentors, peers, sponsors, and your broader network. Your relationships should accelerate your goals, not distract from them. If your network is accidental, your trajectory will be inconsistent.

4. Professional Value Proposition

CEOs clarify what only they can do. For you, that means sharpening your Unique Value Proposition (UVP). What's your "wow factor" that you consistently deliver? What do you consistently bring to the table that makes you stand out?

5. Learning & Adaptability

In business, industries shift and leaders must adapt. Careers work the same way. Commit to lifelong learning. Anticipate change. Adapt before you are required to.

6. Performance & Wellbeing

CEOs must deliver results and sustain themselves for the long haul. For you, that means tracking progress (metrics, milestones) while balancing your physical and mental wellbeing. Burnout kills companies—and careers too. Sustainable performance outperforms short bursts of intensity.

Run It Like a Business

Alex graduated two years ago and landed an analyst role at a fast-growing tech company. At first, he was good at his work—but felt invisible—constantly grinding without recognition or forward progress. He was productive but not positioned.

When Alex reframed himself as the *CEO of You, Inc.*, things began to shift:

- **Personal Operating System:** He blocked time each week for networking and skills practice instead of letting urgent tasks take over.

- **Career Strategy:** He set a 12-month vision: move from analyst to associate product manager.

- **Network Alignment:** He identified two mentors inside the company and scheduled monthly check-ins.

- **Professional Value Proposition:** He crafted a 30-second pitch on how his data skills could help product teams make faster, smarter decisions.

- **Learning & Adaptability:** He enrolled in a product management bootcamp to close his skills gap.

- **Performance & Wellbeing:** He tracked one key metric—how often his work influenced product roadmap decisions.

The lesson: your career doesn't progress by effort alone—it progresses through intentional design.

Six months later, Alex wasn't just working hard—he was working smart, visible, and valued. He was being recognized, expanding his influence, and taking control of his career.

What changed wasn't his talent, but his intentionality. He stopped operating like an employee—and started thinking like an owner.

Exercises for You

- **CEO Audit:** Ask yourself: if my career were an investment opportunity, would I allocate capital to it? Why or why not?

- **Six-Element Check:** Score yourself (1–5) on each element of the CEO of You, Inc. framework. Where are you strong? Where are you falling short?

- **One Strategic Move:** CEOs make bold moves early. Identify one action that meaningfully advances your position in the next 30 days. Write it down.

- **Accountability Partner:** Share your CEO framework. plan with your career center counselor, mentor, or trusted advisor. Invite critique.

Closing Reflection

You don't need the title of CEO to think and act like one. When you step into the role of running your career with clarity and discipline, you shift from reaction to leadership.

Being the CEO of You, Inc. isn't about being perfect. It's about direction, accountability, and ownership. You are your own chief executive. Your career is your enterprise. And your job is to lead accordingly.

As you've seen since Chapter 2, each block closes with The CEO Mindset. Use them as your personal board of directors—guiding you, challenging you, and sparking reflection as you move forward.

Write this on a sticky note:

Keep it on your desk—to remind yourself that you run the business of You, Inc. every day.

The CEO-Mindset

- **Run your career like a company.** CEOs set vision, measure results, and adapt strategy. Do the same with your career—you're responsible for growth and sustainability. Execution distinguishes leaders from participants.

- **Invest your time like capital.** Treat your energy, focus, and habits as limited resources. Direct them toward the roles, skills, and networks that accelerate your growth. Stewardship today determines optionality tomorrow.

- **Clarify your Unique Value Proposition.** CEOs know what only they can deliver. Define your "wow factor" so others remember why they should bet on you.

- **Build your board of directors.** Surround yourself with mentors, peers, and sponsors who will challenge, support, and open doors—just like a CEO relies on advisors.

- **Balance performance and wellbeing.** Long-term results require stamina. Protect your health and mindset the way a CEO protects a company's foundation.

Transition to Unique Value Proposition & Pitch

You've stepped into the CEO seat of your own career. Now it's time to articulate your value proposition—the clear reason others should invest in you.

5

CHAPTER

UNIQUE VALUE PROPOSITION + PITCH

By now, you've clarified your challenges and defined your desired roles. But clarity without differentiation is insufficient—you must demonstrate why *you* are the right fit. That is where the CEO of You, Inc. discipline becomes operational.

As CEO of You, Inc., one of your most important responsibilities is knowing—and communicating—your value. Every company needs a clear value proposition to stand out in a crowded market. The same is true for you. Markets reward differentiation. Employers do the same.

In periods of market contraction or what we earlier described as *layoff fatigue*, applicant pools expand while hiring confidence tightens. Recruiters move faster. Hiring managers look for clarity. When uncertainty rises, ambiguity becomes expensive. If you do not define your Unique Value Proposition (UVP), you default to sameness—and sameness gets overlooked.

Once defined, your UVP becomes a compass. It shapes your résumé, your LinkedIn profile, your networking conversations, and your interviews. Clarity at this level reduces friction in every interaction. It makes you legible to the market.

Why This Block Matters

Your UVP is the differentiator that separates you from others with similar degrees, backgrounds, or years of experience. It clarifies what you consistently deliver and why it matters (see **Figure 5.1**).

CHALLENGES What's blocking my progress right now?	DESIRED ROLE(S) What job roles or functions am I aiming for?	TARGETED COMPANIES + SECTORS What industries or employers am I focusing on?	SKILL/EXPERIENCE GAPS What am I missing today?	STRATEGIC ACTIONS What steps will I take now?
	UNIQUE VALUE PROPOSITION + THE PITCH What's my personal "wow" factor? **3**	ESSENTIAL SKILLS + CAREER VALUES What skills (hard & soft) are required for these roles?	AVAILABLE RESOURCES What resources can I leverage to advance my career?	SUPPORT CHANNELS Who can offer me guidance and support?
SUCCESS INDICATORS What does success look like?		KEY METRICS How will I measure my progress?	CONTINUOUS LEARNING How will I keep expanding my knowledge and skills?	

Figure 5.1: Block 3—Unique Value Proposition + Pitch

But knowing your UVP is only half the equation. Communicating it with confidence is what turns positioning into opportunity. Your UVP answers the silent question every employer is asking: *Why you?*

It goes beyond listing skills. It explains how you solve problems, create value, and bring something distinctive that others at your level may not. Without a UVP, your résumé reads like documentation. With one, it reads like positioning.

Think of your UVP as both compass and amplifier. It keeps you focused internally while making you memorable externally.

The Bullish Flow

This is why *Unique Value Proposition + Pitch* sits at the end of **Part I — Aim** (see **Figure 5.2**).

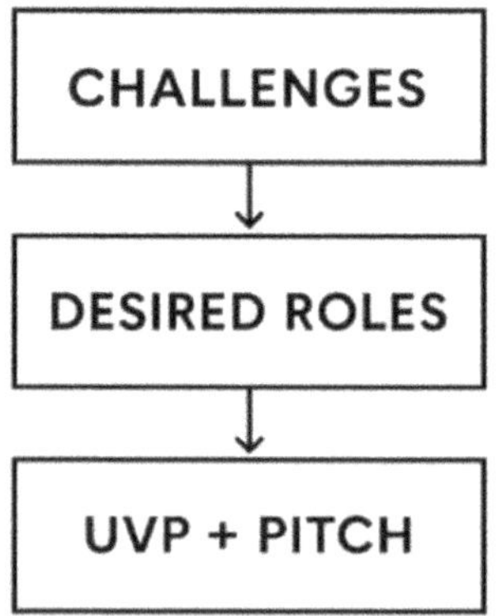

Figure 5.2: Part I of the Bullish Career Canvas

First, challenges clear the fog. Then, desired roles give you direction. Finally, your UVP and pitch sharpen that direction into something employers can recognize and act on. Alignment gets you considered. Differentiation gets you selected.

In volatile markets, that distinction matters more than ever.

How to Work with This Block

Here's how you can break it down into manageable steps as you work through your UVP.

Step 1 — Define Your UVP

Ask yourself: What do I bring that others at my level often don't?

- Is it a rare combination of skills?
- Is strength people consistently notice?
- Is lived experience that informs how you approach problems?
- Is there personal story that connects to my motivation?

Your UVP is rarely just one thing—it's the intersection of strengths, experiences, and values. It should be defensible, not decorative. It should be grounded in evidence, not aspiration.

Step 2 — Draft Your Pitch

A pitch is a short, 30-second statement that answers three questions:

1. Who am I?
2. What do I do best?
3. Where am I heading next?

Your pitch isn't a slogan—it's structured positioning, delivered with clarity and composure. In markets shaped by uncertainty, clarity communicates confidence.

Step 3 — Practice Out Loud

Write it down, then practice saying it to a friend, mentor, or even in front of a mirror. Evaluate: Do you sound genuine? Do you sound confident? Do you sound clear? Would someone want to hear more?

Confidence does not come from memorization. It comes from alignment between what you believe and what you articulate.

UVP Formula

Your UVP can be built using this simple template:

> "I help **[who]** achieve [what] by leveraging **[strengths/skills]**, which results in **[impact/value]**."

Notice the structure: audience, capability, outcome. That sequence matters.

Example (Recent Graduate):

> *"I help small businesses grow their online presence by combining social media strategy with data-driven insights, which results in stronger customer engagement and brand visibility."*

Example (Early-Career Professional):

> *"I help product teams make smarter decisions by turning complex data into clear insights, which results in faster launches and better user experiences."*

If you're struggling to define your UVP, start with a few guiding questions:

- What do I do better or differently than most people at my level?
- Which skills, experiences, or traits do others often compliment me on?
- Can you describe your story and motivation in two to three sentences that feel genuine?
- Can I communicate my pitch out loud in 30 seconds with confidence?

If defining your UVP feels difficult, that's normal. Most professionals have never been taught to articulate value clearly. I recommend that you work closely with a mentor, career coach or advisor. A strong UVP has three qualities:

1. **Clear**: Free of jargon. Anyone should understand it in 10 seconds.
2. **Specific:** Focused on your actual strengths, not vague buzzwords.
3. **Relevant**: Connected to the needs of your target role or industry.

Stand Out or Fade Out

Marcus, a recent graduate in Business Administration, felt stuck. Like many new grads, his résumé looked similar to dozens of his peers—internships, part-time jobs, campus leadership roles. What set Marcus apart was his ability to connect people and ideas.

Marcus' résumé listed coursework and a part-time retail job – full of activity but not differentiation. His LinkedIn headline simply read:

Before: *"Recent Business Administration Graduate | Seeking Opportunities"*

The problem? It said nothing about his value. It described status—not contribution. Recruiters scrolling LinkedIn would pass right by.

When Marcus worked through the *Bullish Career Canvas*, he realized three things:

1. He was naturally strong at analyzing problems and presenting solutions.

2. He enjoyed roles where he could connect with people and influence decisions.

3. His internship project in sales analytics had real impact—helping a local company identify $50K in untapped revenue.

Using the UVP formula, Marcus reframed his story:

> *I help businesses make smarter decisions by combining data analysis with clear communication, so that they can uncover growth opportunities and strengthen client relationships.*

From that, Marcus built his new LinkedIn headline and résumé summary:

After (LinkedIn Headline):

"Business graduate who blends data analysis & communication to uncover growth opportunities | Sales & Marketing Focus."

After (Résumé Summary):

"Business Administration graduate with proven ability to analyze sales data and translate insights into actionable growth strategies. Experienced in building client-facing presentations and uncovering revenue opportunities through data-driven storytelling."

The lesson: if you don't define your value, the market won't either.

The shift was immediate. Notice the shift: Marcus went from invisible to in-demand simply by clarifying and communicating his value.

Within weeks, Marcus received two recruiter messages commenting on his LinkedIn headline alone. He became legible to the market—clear, specific, and easy to understand. His UVP didn't just help him stand out—it positioned him.

Put Your UVP to Work

Your UVP isn't meant to stay hidden in a notebook—it should be front and center where people discover you. Your UVP is the headline, your pitch is the copy, and your results are the proof.

Here's how to put it into action:

- **LinkedIn Headline:** Replace a generic title (e.g., *"Marketing Associate"*) with your UVP.

- o Example: *"Creative marketer who builds campaigns that drive engagement & growth | Skilled in SEO, social, and content strategy."*

Specifically signals competence.

- **LinkedIn About Section:** Expand your UVP into 3–4 sentences that tell your story, highlight strengths, and show impact.

- **Résumé Summary:** Open with your UVP to frame your experiences around value, not just duties.

- **Networking Conversations:** Use your UVP as your 30-second pitch when someone asks, *"So, tell me about yourself?"*

Prove your value by living it across platforms. The more consistent your UVP, the more memorable and credible you become.

Exercises for You

1. **Define Your UVP.** Identify one capability, one strength, and one proof point.

2. **Draft Your Pitch.** Turn your UVP into 2–3 sentences that answer: Who am I? What do I do best? Where am I heading?

3. **Practice.** Deliver it aloud until it feels precise and natural.

4. **Seek Critique.** Share your pitch with a mentor, career counselor, or peer. Ask: "What sticks with you the most?"

5.   **Refine.** Adjust based on feedback until your pitch feels confident and authentic.

Closing Reflection

Your UVP and pitch are your positioning strategy. They're not about being flashy—they're about being clear. When you articulate your value clearly and consistently, you reduce ambiguity.

Like any good CEO, your job is to communicate value clearly and consistently. Once you own your UVP and pitch, you'll notice something powerful: people start to remember you for what you stand for.

Take fifteen minutes to draft your UVP and practice your pitch out loud. It may feel awkward at first—but each repetition builds clarity and confidence.

Write this on a sticky note:

Stick it near your mirror and practice saying it out loud until it feels natural and powerful.

The CEO-Mindset

- **Value beats volume.** CEOs don't compete by being louder—they compete by being clearer. Define your UVP so others know why you matter. Differentiation is strategic, not accidental.

- **Communicate with confidence.** A strong UVP isn't useful if you keep it in your head. Articulate it consistently.

- **Consistency builds credibility.** Align your résumé, LinkedIn, and networking conversations around one clear value story.

- **Make it memorable.** A UVP isn't a slogan—it's a story that sticks because it's authentic, relevant, and impactful. Memorability increases selection probability.

Transition to Fit

You now have the first three blocks of **Part I — AIM**: your challenges, desired roles, and UVP. Together, they form a coherent positioning strategy.

You've built the foundation. Now it's time to test your positioning against the market. **Part II — FIT** begins with targeting the companies and sectors where your value can shine brightest

PART TWO

FIT

6

CHAPTER

TARGETED COMPANIES / SECTORS

A job search without focus becomes activity without direction—you may stay busy, but you never arrive anywhere meaningful. Too often, job seekers substitute volume for strategy: applying broadly across industries without asking whether those companies align with their goals, strengths, or long-term trajectory.

In times shaped by restructuring, cost-cutting, and industry shifts, scattershot applications become even more exhausting. You refresh job boards daily. You apply to roles that are adjacent—but not aligned. You wait. Silence accumulates. Eventually, it begins to feel personal.

Precision changes that.

Targeting specific companies and sectors allows you to invest your energy where it matters most—crafting tailored applications, building meaningful relationships, and preparing to show employers why you are not just qualified, but relevant. Targeting transforms you from an applicant into a contributor.

Fit is not about where you belong—it's about where you can win.

Experience consistently shows this approach works. Focused applications generate higher response rates and uncover "hidden jobs"—roles that never appear publicly but surface through referrals or insider conversations. In uncertain markets, randomness feels safe because it feels active. But opportunity rarely rewards randomness. It rewards alignment.

As shown on **Figure 6.1**, *Bullish Career Canvas*, Block 4 asks:

What industries or employers am I focusing on?

CHALLENGES	DESIRED ROLE(S)	TARGETED COMPANIES + SECTORS	SKILL/EXPERIENCE GAPS	STRATEGIC ACTIONS
What's blocking my progress right now?	What job roles or functions am I aiming for?	What industries or employers am I focusing on? **4**	What am I missing today?	What steps will I take now?
	UNIQUE VALUE PROPOSITION + THE PITCH	ESSENTIAL SKILLS + CAREER VALUES	AVAILABLE RESOURCES	SUPPORT CHANNELS
	What's my personal "wow" factor?	What skills (hard & soft) are required for these roles?	What resources can I leverage to advance my career?	Who can offer me guidance and support?
SUCCESS INDICATORS		KEY METRICS	CONTINUOUS LEARNING	
What does success look like?		How will I measure my progress?	How will I keep expanding my knowledge and skills?	

Figure 6.1: Block 4—Targeted Companies + Sectors

Why this Block Matters

When you target with intention, you gain:

- **Efficiency**: You eliminate roles that dilute your positioning.

- **Stronger positioning**: Your résumé and LinkedIn headline speak directly to what companies need.

- **Access to unposted roles**: Networking with insiders uncovers opportunities before they're posted.

- **Strategic alignment**: Your values and skills line up with the employer's mission and culture.

The alternative is diffusion—energy scattered across markets that were never aligned in the first place. Diffusion breeds frustration. Focus builds momentum.

In environments shaped by layoffs or hiring slowdowns, control feels scarce. Targeting restores a sense of agency. You may not control macroeconomic forces, but you can control where you aim.

How to Work with This Block

Step 1 — Define Your Job Search Vision

Before building a target list, define your market criteria.

- What industries excite you—and why?

- Which business models align with how I want to create value (tech startup, nonprofit, global firm, etc.)?

- Where am I open to working—specific cities, remote, or hybrid?
- What company size best suits my strengths—startup scrappiness, mid-size growth, or enterprise stability?

Clarity at this stage prevents wasted motion later. When the market feels noisy, your criteria become your filter.

Step 2 — Create a Target List (15–20 Companies)

Construct a disciplined list of 15-20 companies. Include:

- **Target companies** (your top picks)
- **Stretch companies** (competitive but worth pursuing)
- **Backup options** (aligned, but more accessible)

This list is not aspirational—it is strategic. It is a working portfolio of opportunity.

Step 3 — Research Your Targets

A list is only as good as the research behind it. Research converts preference into intelligence. Explore:

- Company websites and blogs → mission, culture, products.
- LinkedIn → employees' backgrounds, hiring patterns, alumni connections.
- News alerts → growth, funding rounds, leadership changes.
- Glassdoor, TheMuse, or Fairygodboss → culture, benefits, employee experiences.

- Industry reports → who's growing, merging, or hiring.

In markets experiencing restructuring and AI-driven shifts, intelligence matters more than enthusiasm. Research allows you to move with awareness rather than assumption.

Step 4 — Prioritize and Rank

Not all targets are equal. Rank based on:

- Alignment with your skills and values.

- Growth potential and stability.

- Cultural fit and leadership reputation.

- Practical factors like salary range, benefits, and commute/remote options.

Ranking forces trade-offs. Trade-offs clarify priorities.

Step 5 — Build Connections

Targeting is not just research—it's relationships. Follow company updates to spot timing for outreach. Timing often determines traction. Use LinkedIn to:

- Reach out to alumni or second-degree connections.

- Request informational interviews.

- Follow company updates to spot timing for outreach.

In uncertain markets, referrals matter more. Warm introductions travel farther than cold submissions.

From Activity to Alignment

Jason had just finished his degree in Finance. His early applications were scattered—across banks, startups, consulting firms. After sending over 200 résumés and only one interview, he admitted he didn't know what he was truly aiming for.

After a candid networking conversation, Jason admitted he was lost—and ready to start over.

Using Crunchbase, Jason built a comprehensive list of 15 target companies across two sectors: fintech startups and mid-sized investment firms. He chose them because they valued data skills (his strength), had growth opportunities, and were concentrated in cities he wanted to live in. He targeted markets that aligned with his strengths rather than hoping the market would adjust to him.

From there, Jason researched each company:

- He studied job descriptions on LinkedIn to identify common skills and requirements.

- He read employee reviews on Glassdoor to compare company cultures.

- He set up Google Alerts for his top five firms to stay informed.

- He subscribed to VC News Daily to receive alerts on new startup funding.

The lesson: targeting creates alignment—and alignment drives results.

With this focus, Jason rewrote his résumé and LinkedIn headline around financial modeling + fintech growth insights. He stopped presenting as a generalist and started positioning himself more as a specialist. Specialists are easier to place than generalists.

Within six weeks, Jason landed three interviews—two through applications and one through an alumni referral.

Jason's shift wasn't luck. It was alignment. When he stopped chasing everything, he started attracting the right opportunities.

Exercises for You

1. **Brainstorm**: Identify 20 strategically aligned companies you'd be excited to work for.

2. **Research**: Use LinkedIn, company websites, and news alerts to gather details.

3. **Rank**: Prioritize your top 15 companies based on alignment and opportunity.

4. **Connect**: Reach out to at least two insiders this month.

5. **Track**: Measure conversion rates. Maintain a simple spreadsheet of applications, contacts, and market insights.

Closing Reflection

Your target list is dynamic—it's a living map. As you grow, some companies will drop off, new ones will be added. The goal isn't perfection—it's deliberate focus that moves you forward.

When you know who you are aiming for, everything sharpens—your résumé, your networking, your narrative. Instead of hoping to be discovered, you are intentionally engaging with organizations where your strengths are relevant.

In uncertain environments, clarity is calming. Alignment is energizing.

Write this on a sticky note:

Place it on your laptop—a reminder to stop wasting time on scattershot applications.

Transition into the Periscope

Even with a disciplined target list, you can miss structural shifts in the market. You may see the obvious job postings but overlook the signals that reveal where opportunity is truly emerging. That's where we need a tool that lifts your view above the noise. Your target list sharpens your aim, but even the sharpest aim can miss hidden opportunities. To see beyond the obvious, you need a wider lens. Next, raise the *Career Periscope*.

7

CHAPTER

THE PERISCOPE

Many job seekers confuse activity with progress. High-volume activity feels productive, but in uncertain markets it often produces exhaustion rather than advancement. When headlines are filled with restructuring, AI-driven disruption, and waves of layoffs, it becomes easy to fall into reactive behavior—refreshing job boards, applying broadly, and hoping momentum will build through sheer effort. Unfortunately, effort without direction rarely creates leverage. It creates fatigue.

The *Career Periscope* model introduces a different approach (see **Figure 7.1**). Rather than reacting to what is immediately visible, it elevates your perspective so you can scan for signals before they become obvious to everyone else. Think of a submarine operating beneath the surface. Without a periscope, its visibility is limited to what is directly in front of it. With elevation, even slight elevation, it can scan the horizon and anticipate movement before danger or opportunity becomes unavoidable.

Career navigation works the same way. Without a tool to lift your view, you compete only for what is posted. With a structured lens, you position yourself for what is forming.

In markets shaped by volatility, reacting late means entering crowded applicant pools. Strategic awareness means recognizing patterns early and moving before the crowd gathers. The Periscope is not random browsing. It is disciplined signal detection.

Four Lenses of the Periscope

When you raise the Periscope, you are not scanning aimlessly. You are looking through four deliberate lenses that convert noise into insight:

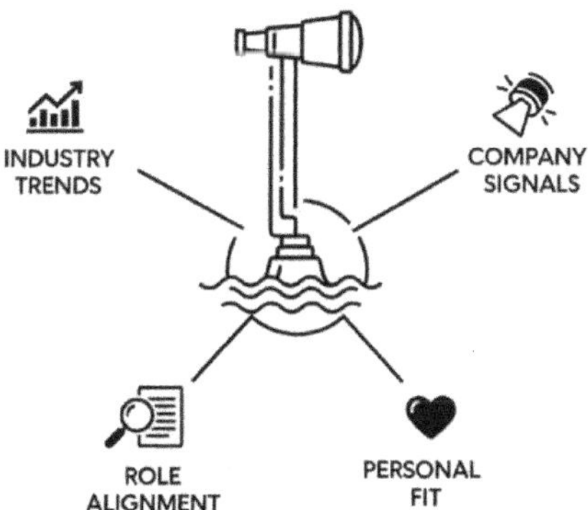

Figure 7.1: Career Periscope Model

The Periscope is not reactive browsing. It is structured signal detection.

Industry Trends

The first lens examines sector-level momentum. Which industries are expanding? Which are consolidating? Where is capital flowing? Where is innovation accelerating?

Periods of disruption do not eliminate opportunity—they redistribute it. As some sectors contract, others accelerate. AI, renewable energy, healthcare innovation, cybersecurity, climate technology—these are examples of sectors where growth often precedes hiring velocity. When you understand macro trends, you reduce surprise. Instead of being destabilized by layoffs in one industry, you recognize where adjacent demand may be increasing.

Trend awareness restores a sense of strategic footing in environments that otherwise feel unpredictable.

Company Signals

The second lens narrows the view from sectors to organizations. Which companies are raising funding, expanding into new markets, launching new products, or making executive hires? These signals often precede hiring waves.

Hiring is rarely random. It follows expansion, capital infusion, product growth, and strategic repositioning. When you learn to measure these signals—through funding announcements, press releases, or leadership changes—you begin to see hiring probability before roles accumulate hundreds of applicants. This awareness allows you to engage earlier and more intentionally.

Role Alignment

The third lens asks a more personal question: Do the roles emerging in these companies align with your Unique Value Proposition, skills, and aspirations? Where do their needs intersect with your strengths?

It is easy, especially in uncertain markets, to pursue roles simply because they are available. The Periscope forces a more disciplined filter. Alignment creates leverage. Misalignment creates friction. When your strengths clearly intersect with market demand, positioning becomes easier and conversations become more compelling.

Personal Fit

The fourth lens addresses sustainability. Do the company's values, culture, and working style align with how you operate best? Can you thrive there—not just survive?

Periods of instability often pressure professionals into prioritizing security alone. But long-term resilience depends on more than income. It depends on alignment with culture, leadership, and values. Layoff fatigue does not only stem from job loss; it also arises from prolonged stress in environments that were never the right fit to begin with. Evaluating fit early protects both performance and wellbeing.

How to Use the Periscope

1. **Scan Weekly**: Schedule a recurring time to scan industry news, LinkedIn updates, and press releases.

2. **Filter**: Drop each signal or opportunity into one of the four lenses. If it fails multiple lenses, it's noise—not worth your time.

3. **Prioritize**: Place your top 10–15 companies at the center of your Periscope view. Concentration creates leverage.

4. **Act**: Translate signals into targeted outreach, applications, and relationship-building.

The Periscope is not complete until it produces measurable movement.

Vision Creates Advantage

Aisha had been working in marketing for three years and wanted to transition into the tech sector—but didn't know where to start.

After a few 1-on-1 coaching sessions, I introduced Aisha to the *Career Periscope* model. Once she applied the Periscope framework, her search shifted:

- **Industry Trends** → Noticed rapid growth in B2B SaaS.

- **Company Signals** → Flagged Series B startups with new marketing budgets.

- **Role Alignment** → Found job descriptions calling for her digital campaign skills.

- **Personal Fit** → Prioritized companies promoting diversity and remote work.

Aisha's search narrowed, but her probability increased. Within two months, she focused her search on 12 companies. She reached out to insiders, tailored her résumé, and landed interviews at two software companies.

The lesson: focus comes from seeing signals early—and filtering out everything else.

The *Career Periscope* didn't just help her spot opportunities—it helped her filter out noise and remain confident in her direction.

Aisha's advantage wasn't volume—it was signal recognition. She positioned early where other reacted late. She raised her view—while everyone else kept playing the same game.

Exercises for You

1. **Construct Your Periscope Framework**: Draw four quadrants: Trends, Signals, Alignment, Fit.

2. **May Companies Against Lenses**: Place each target company into the quadrant(s) it matches.

3. **Prioritize**: Choose your top 10–15 based on overlap across quadrants.

4. **Act**: Initiate one high-quality outreach or application weekly based on your Periscope insights.

Closing Reflection

The Career Periscope is designed to lift you above chaos. It replaces emotional reaction with structured awareness. Instead of competing solely in crowded applicant pools, you are scanning strategically, filtering intelligently, and acting deliberately.

The Periscope shows the horizon, but clarity also depends on what you bring to the table—your skills, values, and drive.

Write this on a sticky note:

Place it where you work. Every time you're tempted to apply impulsively, pause and scan first.

The CEO-Mindset

- **Raise your view.** CEOs don't just look at today's numbers—they scan for market shifts. Use your Periscope to see beyond the obvious. Strategic awareness precedes strategic action.

- **Filter the noise.** Not every opportunity deserves your energy. Drop signals into your four lenses and focus only where alignment is real.

- **Translate signals into measurable moves.** CEOs don't stop at data—they turn signals into strategy. You should too.

- **Move before the market.** Acting early on signals gives you a head start while others are still reacting.

Transition to Essential Skills & Career Values

You now have elevation. You can see where opportunity is forming.

Next, we anchor awareness with capability: *Essential Skills + Career Values*—the backpack and compass you carry into every opportunity. Because even the clearest horizon requires preparation to reach it.

8

CHAPTER

ESSENTIAL SKILLS + CAREER VALUES

Every career journey rests on two forces: the skills you carry in your backpack and the values that serve as your compass. Skills equip you for the climb. Values determine whether you are climbing the right mountain. Without both, you risk either being unprepared for the ascent or reaching a destination that looks impressive from the outside but feels hollow from within.

In today's labor market, employers are not hiring résumés—they are hiring individuals who can deliver results and contribute to culture. That distinction matters more than ever. As organizations navigate restructuring, automation, and rapid industry shifts, they look for people who are not only capable, but adaptable and aligned. Companies spend enormous energy clarifying their core values—principles like innovation, integrity, collaboration, customer-first thinking—because they understand that culture drives performance over time.

As a job seeker, you must apply the same rigor to yourself.

Why this Block Matters

Block 5 of the *Bullish Career Canvas* asks you to define both your essential skills and your career values (see **Figure 8.1**). This is not a soft reflection exercise. It is a strategic inventory.

Without clarity, you may accept a role that looks impressive on paper but feels draining in practice. In volatile markets, it is tempting to prioritize security alone—salary, title, brand recognition. But security without alignment often leads to quiet dissatisfaction. Over time, that dissatisfaction compounds into disengagement or burnout.

When the market feels unstable, alignment becomes even more critical. Skills keep you employable. Values keep you energized.

CHALLENGES What's blocking my progress right now?	DESIRED ROLE(S) What job roles or functions am I aiming for?	TARGETED COMPANIES + SECTORS What industries or employers am I focusing on?	SKILL/EXPERIENCE GAPS What am I missing today?	STRATEGIC ACTIONS What steps will I take now?
	UNIQUE VALUE PROPOSITION + THE PITCH What's my personal "wow" factor?	ESSENTIAL SKILLS + CAREER VALUES What skills (hard & soft) are required for these roles? **5**	AVAILABLE RESOURCES What resources can I leverage to advance my career?	SUPPORT CHANNELS Who can offer me guidance and support?
SUCCESS INDICATORS What does success look like?		KEY METRICS How will I measure my progress?	CONTINUOUS LEARNING How will I keep expanding my knowledge and skills?	

Figure 8.1: Block 5—Essential Skills + Career Values

Why Skills Alone Aren't Enough

Early-career professionals often over-index on technical skills—certifications, platforms, credentials, tools. These matter. They create entry. They open doors. But credentials create access; behavior creates trajectory.

Employers increasingly evaluate essential transferable skills: communication, adaptability, collaboration, problem-solving, emotional intelligence. As automation reshapes work and AI absorbs repetitive tasks, social and cognitive capabilities are rising in importance (see **Figure 8.2**). Technical fluency may differentiate you initially, but your ability to think critically, communicate clearly, and collaborate effectively determines your long-term growth.

However, even possessing the right skill stack does not guarantee sustainability. If your environment contradicts your values, your performance will eventually suffer. For example, if you value collaboration but work in a hyper-competitive culture, the friction will drain you. If you value stability but operate in constant chaos, stress will accumulate.

Skills may get you hired. Values determine whether you thrive.

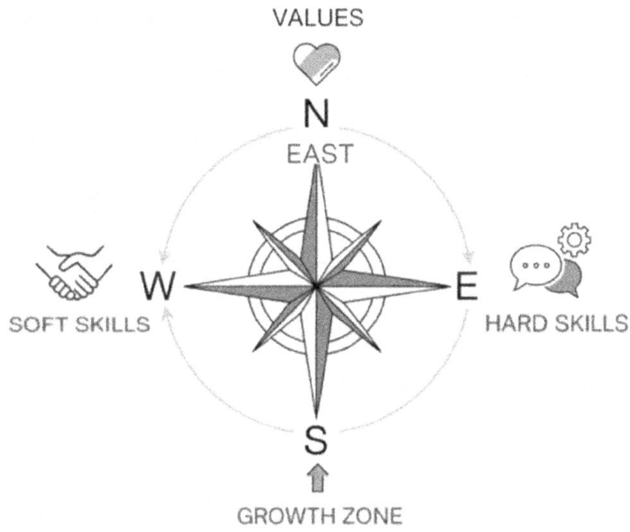

Figure 8.2: Professional Compass

The Barbell Strategy: Balancing Stability and Growth

In uncertain markets, one of the most common mistakes professionals make is overcorrecting in a single direction. Some pursue only stability—choosing safe roles, familiar skills, and predictable paths. Others chase only upside—jumping into new tools, industries, or risks without a foundation.

Both approaches create fragility.

A concept from the world of investing, popularized by Nassim Nicholas Taleb, offers a more resilient approach: the *Barbell Strategy*. Instead of choosing between safety and risk, the barbell combines both—intentionally and strategically.

Applied to your career, the *Barbell Strategy* means balancing two forces (see **Figure 8.3**):

- **Stability:** the skills, experiences, and roles that keep you employable and grounded

- **Upside:** the experiments, stretch opportunities, and new capabilities that expand your future potential

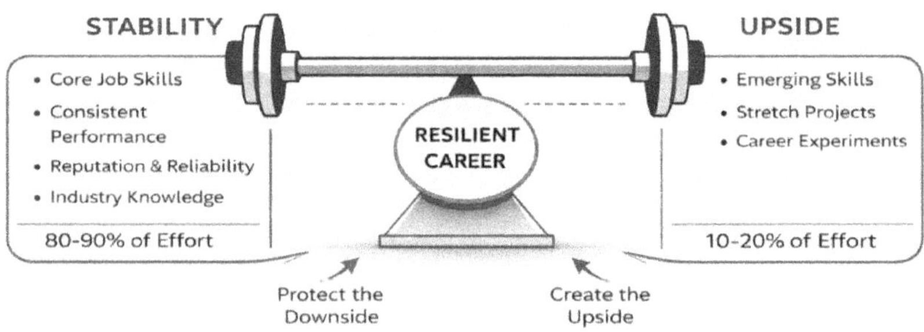

Figure 8.3: The Barbell Career Strategy

Most of your effort should be anchored in stability. This includes mastering the core skills required for your role, delivering consistent performance, and building a reputation for reliability. These are your anchors. They protect your downside and preserve your market value. They ensure that no matter how the market shifts, you remain valuable.

But stability alone is not enough. Without intentional upside, your growth eventually plateaus.

That is where the second side of the barbell comes in.

A smaller portion of your effort should be allocated to high-upside activities—learning emerging skills, exploring adjacent roles, contributing to new projects, or building something outside your immediate responsibilities. These are not random actions—they are deliberate bets on your future.

For example, a marketing manager may continue to execute core campaigns (stability) while learning data analytics or AI tools on the side (upside). A software engineer may deliver within their current stack while contributing to open-source projects or experimenting with new frameworks. A student may focus on coursework while building a portfolio that signals applied capability.

The goal is not balance in equal measure. It is balance in purpose.

Stability protects you. Upside expands you.

When you neglect stability, you become exposed. When you neglect upside, you become stagnant. The barbell ensures you are neither fragile nor stuck.

This approach also connects directly to your values.

If you value growth, the upside side of the barbell becomes essential. If you value stability, the foundation becomes non-negotiable. The key is not choosing one over the other—it is designing a career that honors both.

The lesson: build stability with one hand—and upside with the other.

The Role of Career Values

Values act as your internal filter. They determine which opportunities deserve your energy and which will quietly erode it. Without defined values, you default to external validation—salary, prestige, promotion speed—while ignoring internal sustainability.

Your values shape how you define success. They influence whether you feel energized at the end of the day or depleted. Growth, autonomy, creativity, stability, collaboration, purpose— each individual arranges these differently. There is no universally correct hierarchy. There is only alignment or misalignment.

When your values align with your workplace, engagement feels natural. When they do not, friction becomes chronic. That friction is subtle at first. It shows up as fatigue, irritability, or quiet doubt. Over time, it compounds. In environments already strained by uncertainty and organizational change, misalignment amplifies stress.

Alignment produces energy. Misalignment produces friction.

For college students, identifying non-negotiables is often a process of discovery. Many are still experimenting with environments and roles. That is normal. The key is to observe patterns. What energizes you in projects or internships? What frustrates you? What environments bring out your best work?

For professionals, the picture sharpens with experience. After two or three years, patterns emerge. You begin to recognize which conditions allow you to perform at your best—and which quietly diminish you. Your compass grows clearer with exposure.

My Compass

Maia was in her second year at a large consulting firm. It was her first job out of college. On paper, her career looked strong: she had mastered Excel modeling, presented to clients, and managed tight deadlines. Maia had been progressing well and received strong reviews from her manager, but something felt off.

At first, Maia assumed it was about her skill set. Maybe she just needed another certification or more technical training. But as she reflected more deeply, she realized the real issue wasn't what she *could* do — it was where she was applying it.

The firm prized individual performance, billable hours, and competition for promotion. Maia, however, valued collaboration, mentorship, and creativity.

Maia's skills were not the problem. The environment was misaligned with her values.

The lesson: when your environment conflicts with your values, your performance will always be constrained.

Once she recognized this, her strategy shifted. She began targeting organizations that explicitly emphasized teamwork, innovation, and cross-functional collaboration. Within months, she transitioned into a product marketing role at a mid-sized technology company.

The skills she had built in consulting remained relevant. But now they were deployed in an environment that reinforced her values rather than undermined them. The impact was immediate. Her satisfaction increased, but more importantly, her performance amplified. Alignment did not just improve her mood—it amplified her impact.

For the first time, she felt not only capable—but grounded.

Working With This Block--Essential Skills + Career Values

Conduct a Skills + Values audit.

- **Skills:** Which hard skills create measurable impact? Which transferable skills (communication, leadership, adaptability) consistently surface in feedback?

- **Values:** Which conditions allow you to perform at your best? Which are non-negotiable? (e.g., growth, flexibility, collaboration, integrity).

- **Fit:** Where do your capabilities intersect with environments that reinforce your values?

Document this in writing. Vague awareness is not strategic clarity. A written inventory becomes your reference point when evaluating opportunities. Just as organizations publish values to guide decision-making, you must define yours to steer your career deliberately. "

In volatile markets, clarity reduces reactivity. When you know both what you can do and what you stand for, you make decisions from strength rather than urgency.

Closing Reflection

Skills open doors. Values determine whether you build a sustainable career inside them. By treating your skills as your backpack and your values as your compass, you equip yourself not just to advance—but to endure.

In uncertain markets, endurance matters.

Write this on a sticky note:

Place it where you make career decisions—to check alignment taking on new opportunities. Test both sides of the equation.

The CEO-Mindset

- **Hire yourself twice.** CEOs hire for skills but retain for values. Do the same—choose roles where both align.

- **Balance hard and soft.** Technical skills get you noticed; transferable skills (communication, adaptability, problem-solving) keep you growing.

- **Lead with values.** Companies publish theirs to guide decisions. You should define yours to steer your career.

- **Longevity is built on alignment, no ambition alone.** Skills open the door, but values keep you engaged, energized, and in it for the long haul. Alignment sustains performance over time.

Transition to Skills & Experience Gaps

Now that you understand your capabilities and operating principles, it is time to examine where you are under-leveraged.

Every path contains gaps. In the next chapter, you will use the *Bullish Gap Bridge* to convert those gaps into deliberate growth.

9

CHAPTER

SKILL/EXPERIENCE GAPS

You have taken stock of your skills and clarified the values that guide your decisions. But awareness alone does not create advancement. The next CEO-level question is unavoidable: *What is missing?*

In uncertain markets—where industries restructure, technologies evolve rapidly, and roles change faster than job descriptions—gaps become more visible. High performers do not avoid that visibility. They lean into it. They diagnose early so they are not surprised later.

This is the focus of Block 6 in the *Bullish Career Canvas* (see **Figure 9.1**). To reach your desired role, you must clearly identify the distance between where you are today and where you want to be tomorrow. That distance is not a verdict. It is information.

Gaps typically fall into three categories:

- **Technical:** missing credentials, tools, certifications
- **Experiential:** limited scope, ownership, or leadership exposure
- **Contextual:** unfamiliarity with industry language, workflows, or market dynamics

When markets tighten, hiring managers become more precise. When markets expand, expectations still rise. In both conditions, clarity about your gaps prevents emotional overreaction and reactive decision-making.

Gaps are not threats. They are strategic indicators.

CHALLENGES	DESIRED ROLE(S)	TARGETED COMPANIES + SECTORS	SKILL/EXPERIENCE GAPS	STRATEGIC ACTIONS
What's blocking my progress right now?	What job roles or functions am I aiming for?	What industries or employers am I focusing on?	What am I missing today? **6**	What steps will I take now?
	UNIQUE VALUE PROPOSITION + THE PITCH — What's my personal "wow" factor?	**ESSENTIAL SKILLS + CAREER VALUES** — What skills (hard & soft) are required for these roles?	**AVAILABLE RESOURCES** — What resources can I leverage to advance my career?	**SUPPORT CHANNELS** — Who can offer me guidance and support?
SUCCESS INDICATORS What does success look like?	**KEY METRICS** How will I measure my progress?		**CONTINUOUS LEARNING** How will I keep expanding my knowledge and skills?	

Figure 9.1: Block 6—Skill/Experience Gaps

Why This Block Matters

Too many job seekers get blindsided when recruiters or hiring managers ask, "What experience do you have with X?" and realize they can't give a confident answer. Others land roles that look good on paper but quickly discover they lack the depth to succeed.

By addressing skill and experience gaps directly, you:

- **Strengthen credibility**: You can demonstrate readiness by showing how you're closing gaps.

- **Reframe weaknesses**: Instead of avoiding shortcomings, you position them as active learning goals.

- **Avoid surprises**: You see challenges ahead of time and design a plan to address them.

- **Accelerate growth**: You target the gaps that matter most for your next role, not just "any" role.

In volatile markets, disciplined preparation reduces anxiety. The unknown becomes measurable. The measurable becomes manageable.

The Bullish Gap Bridge

The *Bullish Gap Bridge* borrows from strategic planning disciplines. It forces contrast between your current capability and your target expectation—and then builds an intentional path between the two (see **Figure 9.2**).

Clarity emerges from contrast. When your present state and desired state sit side by side, action becomes visible.

The *Bullish Gap Bridge* asks four essential questions:

1. **Where am I now?**
   - Which skills and experiences do I already possess?

- Which strengths consistently generate results?
- Which values are being honored in my current role?

2. **Where do I want to be?**

- Which skills are required for the roles I'm targeting?
- Which experiences are repeatedly listed in job descriptions?
- Which values must exist in my future workplace for alignment?

3. **What is the gap?**

- Which capabilities are missing today?
- Where do I lack depth, ownership, or exposure?
- Which trade-offs might compromised my values if I pursue the wrong path?

4. **How will I bridge it?**

- What resources (mentors, training, stretch projects) can help close the gap?
- What deliberate steps can I take within the next 30-90 days?
- How will I measure progress?

The power of the Bridge is structural honesty. By breaking a complex challenge into four questions, it turns uncertainty into a roadmap. Instead of feeling overwhelmed by everything you *don't* have yet, you see a clear path forward: what's in place, what's missing, and how you'll close the distance.

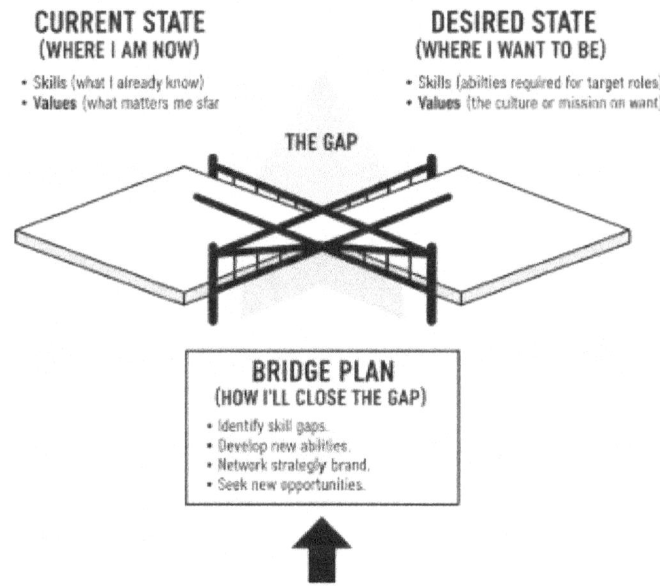

Figure 9.2: Bullish Gap Bridge

The objective is not perfection. It's measurable advancement. Every deliberate step you take across the bridge moves you closer to your career goals.

The Analyst's Leap

Three years into his role as a data analyst at a healthcare company, Diego felt tension building. He enjoyed analytics—but he wanted to transition into product management within health tech. The ambition was clear. The evidence was not.

His résumé demonstrated deep technical fluency—SQL, reporting, dashboards—but showed no ownership of product decisions, no roadmap planning, and no cross-functional leadership. In a competitive job market, aspiration alone would not carry him across.

When Diego mapped his *Bullish Gap Bridge*, the contrast clarified his path forward.

- **Current State:** Strong analytical skills, precision in reporting, trusted contributor on data insights. He valued impact and precision.

- **Desired State:** Product manager role requiring cross-functional leadership, customer research exposure, and roadmap ownership. Collaboration and innovation were central.

- **The Gap:** No direct product lifecycle ownership. Limited exposure to customer interviews. Minimal influence on product prioritization decisions.

- **Bridge Plan:** Enrolled in a product management certification program. He requested to shadow customer discovery calls. He volunteered for a cross-functional initiative that required stakeholder coordination beyond analytics.

The lesson: you don't close gaps by intention—you close them through evidence.

Within twelve months, Diego was no longer "a data analyst who wanted to be a product manager." He had real product stories. He could articulate trade-offs, customer insights, and roadmap considerations. His résumé evolved—but more importantly, his story matured.

When Diego interviewed, he did not apologize for his gaps—he explained how he had bridged them.

Bridged gaps become interview leverage.

Exercises for You

Approach your gaps with discipline rather than defensiveness.

1. **Gap Inventory:** Identify three capability gaps tied directly to your desired role—not generic improvements, but role-specific deficiencies.

2. **Timeline Analysis:** Separate near-term gaps (skills you can strengthen within six to twelve months) from structural gaps that require multi-year development.

3. **Interview Reframe:** Draft a proactive statement demonstrating initiative. For example: *"I recognized that I needed deeper project leadership experience, so I volunteered for a cross-functional initiative and enrolled in a structured certification to build that exposure."*

4. **Bridge Commitment:** Document one deliberate step you will execute this month. Progress compounds through small, consistent advancement.

When you convert gaps into plans, fear decreases. Direction increases.

Closing Reflection

Your skills and values serve as your compass. Gaps are the terrain between you and your destination. Ignoring them does not make the climb easier—it makes it unpredictable.

In markets shaped by disruption and rapid change, proactive gap management signals maturity. Hiring managers are not searching for perfection. They are searching for readiness, adaptability, and forward momentum.

When you speak about your growth with clarity and ownership, you demonstrate leadership potential.

Write this on a sticky note:

Place it where you plan your development. Let it remind you that gaps are indicators of growth, not excuses for stagnation.

The CEO-Mindset

Strategic leaders analyze gaps in their organizations and build deliberate solutions. You must apply the same logic to your career.

- **Treat gaps are data.** CEOs study gaps in their business to plan growth. Treat your career gaps the same way—measure them, then act.

- **Frame them proactively.** Weaknesses aren't liabilities if you frame them as learning goals and show progress.

- **Bridge them deliberately.** Random efforts won't close meaningful gaps. Build a clear plan that connects where you are to where you want to go. Build structural solutions, not temporary fixes.

- **Articulate the climb.** In interviews, articulate not just what you've achieved, but how you've closed the distance from where you started.

Transition to Action

You have diagnosed the distance and begun constructing your bridge. Now we moved from diagnosis to acceleration.

Part III — ACTION focuses on leverage: the resources and systems that compound your progress and shorten the distance between where you are and where you are going.

PART THREE

ACTION

10

CHAPTER

AVAILABLE RESOURCES

By now, you have clarified your challenges, sharpened your value, and identified your gaps. But even the clearest plan stalls without fuel—and fuel, in career terms, is leverage. Leverage is not about working longer hours or pushing harder. It is about using the right inputs to multiply your effort. In the *Bullish Career Canvas*, Block 7 asks a deceptively simple question: *What resources can I leverage to advance my career?* (see **Figure 10.1**).

Resources are performance multipliers. Two candidates with identical résumés can experience radically different outcomes based on how effectively they deploy what is around them—who they learn from, what tools they use, and how intentionally they invest their time and money. The difference is rarely talent alone. It is strategy.

In uncertain markets, where competition intensifies and change accelerates, trying to do everything alone is exhausting. Yet many job seekers fall into that trap. Some believe the only path forward is relentless hustle or expensive credentials. Others swing in the opposite direction, collecting endless free resources but never committing to deeper investments that accelerate results. Both extremes create imbalance.

In reality, resources come in layers. Some are free and already within reach. Others require financial commitment but dramatically compress learning curves. The real discipline lies in knowing when to explore broadly at low cost and when to invest narrowly with conviction.

CHALLENGES	DESIRED ROLE(S)	TARGETED COMPANIES + SECTORS	SKILL/EXPERIENCE GAPS	STRATEGIC ACTIONS
What's blocking my progress right now?	What job roles or functions am I aiming for?	What industries or employers am I focusing on?	What am I missing today?	What steps will I take now?

UNIQUE VALUE PROPOSITION + THE PITCH	ESSENTIAL SKILLS + CAREER VALUES	AVAILABLE RESOURCES	SUPPORT CHANNELS
What's my personal "wow" factor?	What skills (hard & soft) are required for these roles?	What resources can I leverage to advance my career? **7**	Who can offer me guidance and support?

SUCCESS INDICATORS	KEY METRICS	CONTINUOUS LEARNING
What does success look like?	How will I measure my progress?	How will I keep expanding my knowledge and skills?

Figure 10.1: Block 7—Available Resources

Why This Block Matters

Resources reduce friction. They shorten trial-and-error cycles. They prevent you from reinventing what others have already refined.

A single conversation with the right mentor can redirect months of confusion. A focused course can accelerate a skill that would otherwise take a year to develop. A well-timed introduction can open doors that dozens of cold applications cannot.

Students who actively leverage career centers, alumni networks, and faculty mentors consistently gain traction faster than those who only apply online. Professionals who allocate budget toward targeted certifications or coaching often move ahead of peers who rely solely on improvisation.

The difference is not intensity—it is leverage.

Intensity without leverage produces exhaustion. Leverage produces acceleration.

When you think strategically about resources, you stop guessing and start investing effort where return is highest.

Resource Matrix

To make this practical, let's borrow a familiar tool from business strategy to career development: the quadrant. By plotting resources across two dimensions—**Cost (Free vs. Paid)** and **Format (People vs. Tools)**—you see the full picture of what's available (see **Figure 10.2**).

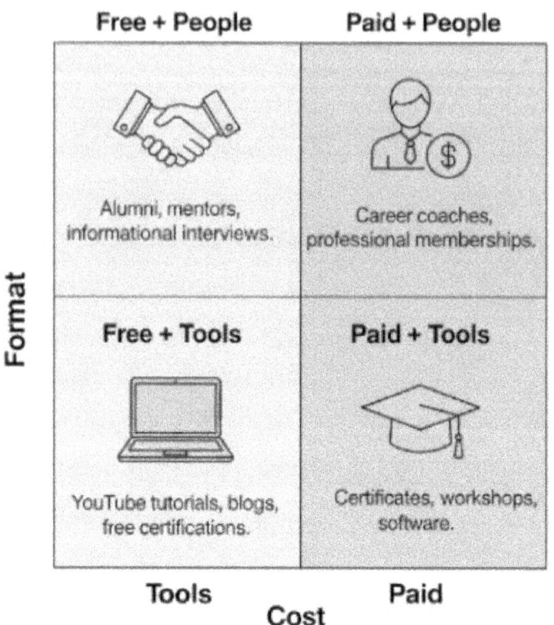

Figure 10.2: Resource Matrix

- **Free + Tools** → YouTube tutorials, Coursera audits, blogs, newsletters, podcasts, free résumé templates, career center libraries.

- **Paid + Tools** → Certificates, bootcamps, workshops, assessments, coaching platforms, professional software.

- **Free + People** → Informational interviews, alumni networks, professors, mentors, peer study groups, LinkedIn communities.

- **Paid + People** → Career coaches, masterminds, professional memberships, structured mentorship programs.

Most job seekers lean too heavily into one quadrant. Some overinvest in tools—accumulating credentials without building relationships. Others network extensively but neglect skill depth. Growth becomes uneven.

The Resource Matrix forces balance.

The most strategic approach is sequencing: explore broadly at low cost, validate direction through people, and then invest deliberately once clarity increases.

Exploration without commitment creates career drift. Commitment without validation creates regret. Sequencing creates traction.

Free First, Invest Smart

Sarah had just graduated with a communications degree and wanted to get into digital marketing. She wasn't sure where to begin. Her first instinct was to enroll in a $2,000 online bootcamp program recommended by a colleague.

The program's promise of a "fast track" to a great job in as little as 90 days was tempting—but it also felt risky. Before she clicked "enroll," she paused and mapped her options using the Resource Matrix.

- **Free + Tools:** Completed Google's free Digital Marketing modules and HubSpot Academy certifications.

- **Free + People:** Joined her university's alumni LinkedIn group and scheduled three informational interviews with alumni working in marketing. One conversation revealed that portfolio work mattered more than expensive credentials at entry level a critical insight that changed her approach.

- **Paid + Tools:** After confirming her interest, she invested $300 in an advanced SEO course that included real-world projects.

- **Paid + People:** Scheduled a few sessions with a career center counselor at her alma mater to refine her résumé and mock interviews.

The lesson: validate direction before you invest in it.

Within four months, Sarah had a credible portfolio, refined positioning, and clarity about her direction. She secured a digital marketing associate role without overinvesting prematurely.

Sarah's breakthrough wasn't luck—it was sequencing. She explored for free, validated with people, and then invested smartly. She validated direction before deploying capital.

Sarah's example shows how starting with free resources and layering in smart investments can create traction without overspending.

But not everyone takes this balanced approach. Some professionals lean too heavily in one direction—investing too much in tools or credentials while neglecting the people who can open doors. That's where David's story comes in.

Skills Open Doors, People Unlock Them

David, an early-career software engineer, took the opposite path—he over-indexed on Paid + Tools. He lacked internship experience, so he spent thousands on specialized online courses to build his credentials alongside his technical degree—but he neglected networking.

David's résumé was stacked with certifications, yet he struggled to get callbacks from recruiters because no one in his industry who he was.

Once David rebalanced—joining online communities, reaching out to alumni, and investing in a professional association—things began to shift. He joined LinkedIn groups like *Software Developers Network* and *Machine Learning & AI Professionals*, discovered GitHub and began contributing to open-source projects.

By actively participating in these communities, David built meaningful connections in the software engineering world. Those connections soon turned into referrals that opened doors. David didn't lack skills—he lacked visibility.

The lesson: tools sharpen capability. People unlock opportunity. Without both, progress stalls.

Sarah and David's journeys highlight the spectrum: one sequenced her resources strategically, the other over-invested in tools before discovering the power of people. Both remind us that balance is everything.

How to Work with This Block

Begin by auditing your existing capital. Identify tools and relationships already available to you—many are closer than you think. Career centers, alumni databases, mentors, online communities, and free educational platforms often go underutilized.

Next, define your investment threshold. What justifies financial commitment? Alignment should precede spending. If your direction is unclear, explore first. If your direction is confirmed, invest strategically.

Diversify inputs. Ensure you are developing both capability (tools) and access (people). Overreliance on one creates stagnation.

Establish a resource budget—not only in dollars, but in time. Even fifteen intentional minutes per day invested in learning or outreach compounds over months.

Finally, measure return. Did this course produce skill depth? Did that conversation lead to clarity or introductions? Resource strategy, like business strategy, requires feedback loops.

Exercises for You

1. **Build Your Matrix:** List at least three resources in each quadrant.

2. **Low-Cost Validation:** Engage two free tools and two free conversations before any major paid investment.

3. **Strategic Investment:** Identify one high-conviction paid aligned with your 90-day goals.

4. **ROI Check:** After 30 days, review to assess progress and recalibrate if needed.

If your matrix is unbalanced, correct it. Growth requires diversified leverage.

Closing Reflection

Resources are the multipliers of your career. They expand what you can learn, who you can reach, and how fast you can grow. But the secret isn't just access—it's strategy.

Think of your resources like fuel. Some are abundant and free, like oxygen. Others require deliberate investment, like premium gas. The goal is not to choose one over the other, but to blend them thoughtfully so your progress remains steady and sustainable.

When you approach resources strategically, you reduce waste—of time, energy, and money. You stop chasing everything and begin investing intentionally.

Write this on a sticky note:

Place it where you make decisions about courses, coaching or memberships—a reminder to tap into what's already around you before spending on what's not.

The CEO-Mindset

Strategic leaders do not rely solely on effort. They deploy resources that multiply effort. Apply the same logic to your career.

- **Invest in capability and access simultaneously.** Courses sharpen skills, but relationships open doors. Both matter.

- **Sequence exploration before commitment.** Explore free resources first, validate with mentors, then invest where it counts.

- **Track return on time and capital.** Just like CEOs track returns, monitor which resources deliver real value—skills gained, interviews landed, clarity achieved.

Transition to Strategic Actions

You've stocked your toolkit with people and tools. Resources without execution produce no return. Next, we convert leverage into execution. Chapter 11 introduces Strategic Actions—the deliberate moves that turn preparation into momentum.

11

CHAPTER

STRATEGIC ACTIONS

At this point, you have clarified your challenges, mapped your desired roles, sharpened your value proposition, identified your gaps, and organized your resources. But here is the uncomfortable truth: none of it produces change unless you act.

Strategy without execution is intellectual comfort. It feels productive because it gives you a sense of control. But clarity only compounds when it is tested in motion.

This is where many job seekers stall. They refine their résumé endlessly. They research companies for weeks. They tell themselves they will apply "once everything is perfect." In volatile markets—where layoffs dominate headlines and competition feels intense—perfection becomes a form of protection. If you never apply, you never risk rejection.

But protection is not progress.

Clarity does not emerge from thinking alone. It emerges from doing, observing, and adjusting. Just as startups scale by launching, testing, and iterating, your career advances when you take deliberate action and learn from the feedback.

That's why Block 8 of the *Bullish Career Canvas* asks: *What steps will you take now?* (See **Figure 11.1**).

CHALLENGES What's blocking my progress right now?	DESIRED ROLE(S) What job roles or functions am I aiming for?	TARGETED COMPANIES + SECTORS What industries or employers am I focusing on?	SKILL/EXPERIENCE GAPS What am I missing today?	STRATEGIC ACTIONS What steps will I take now? **8**
	UNIQUE VALUE PROPOSITION + THE PITCH What's my personal "wow" factor?	ESSENTIAL SKILLS + CAREER VALUES What skills (hard & soft) are required for these roles?	AVAILABLE RESOURCES What resources can I leverage to advance my career?	SUPPORT CHANNELS Who can offer me guidance and support?
SUCCESS INDICATORS What does success look like?	KEY METRICS How will I measure my progress?		CONTINUOUS LEARNING How will I keep expanding my knowledge and skills?	

Figure 11.1: Block 8—Strategic Actions

Why This Block Matters

Strategic actions are the bridge between preparation and results. Without them, you stay in theory mode — busy, informed, and stuck. With them, you create forward motion.

When you execute strategically, you:

- **Turn ideas into evidence**: employers respond to demonstrated momentum, not intention.

- **Generate confidence through momentum**: one action sparks the next, building confidence and visibility.

- **Collect data**: each outreach, application, or project gives you feedback on what's working.

- **Build visible traction**: instead of betting everything on one big leap, you test and adjust as you go.

In uncertain markets, action reduces helplessness. It replaces speculation with signal. Every deliberate step creates feedback that thinking alone cannot provide.

This block is your launchpad. The goal is not perfection; it's progression.

The MVP Framework for Career Actions

Borrowed from the startup world, the MVP (Minimum Viable Product) mindset applies iterative execution to career strategy. Startups do not wait until every feature is flawless before launching. They release something functional, gather feedback, refine, and scale.

Your career requires the same discipline.

The *MVP Framework for Career Actions* has four steps (see **Figure 11.2**):

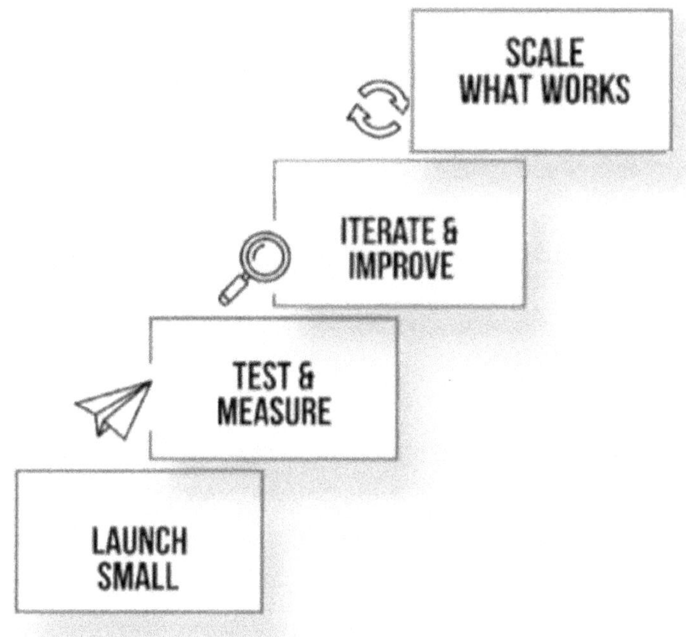

Figure 11.2: MVP Framework for Career Actions

1. **Launch Small**

   Initiate one targeted action immediately—one tailored application, one strategic outreach, one intentional conversation. The action should be meaningful but manageable.

2. **Test & Measure**

   Observe the response. Did someone reply? Did you secure an interview? Did the conversation clarify your positioning? Silence is data. Rejection is data. Engagement is data.

3. **Iterate & Improve**

   Refine based on feedback. Adjust your résumé structure. Strengthen your pitch. Narrow your target list. Small adjustments compound over time.

4. **Scale What Works**

   When traction appears, expand deliberately. Apply to more roles of similar alignment. Deepen relationships in productive networks. Reinforce the strategies generating response.

The framework prevents two extremes: paralysis and chaos.

Frameworks are useful, but they come alive when you see them in practice. To show how the *MVP Framework for Career Actions* works, let's look at two job seekers who approached action in very different ways—and what their outcomes can teach us. Here's what this looks like for Elena.

From Stuck to Motion

Elena, a recent MBA graduate, wanted to break into strategy consulting. For weeks, she kept polishing her résumé and reading about firms—but wasn't applying. *"I'll start when I'm fully ready,"* she told herself.

Underneath that statement was fear.

When she applied the MVP Framework, she shifted from contemplation to execution.

- **Launch Small:** She initiated one outreach to an alum at a top firm for an informational interview.

- **Test & Measure:** The alum gave feedback that her résumé buried her strongest skills.

- **Iterate & Improve:** She restructured her résumé around problem-solving and client impact.

- **Scale What Works:** Encouraged, she applied to five firms and scheduled three more alumni conversations.

The lesson: clarity doesn't come from waiting—it comes from action.

Within two months, Elena secured multiple interviews. The breakthrough wasn't her résumé alone—it was motion.

Each step gave Elena new data, new confidence, and new direction. That's the real power of strategic actions—they create feedback loops that thinking alone cannot provide. Her breakthrough was not refinement—it was execution.

Elena's example shows how even small, intentional steps can create momentum when guided by strategy. But there's another side to the coin. Motion produced signal. Signal produced adjustment. Adjustment produced traction.

While some job seekers hesitate and delay, others rush headfirst into action without direction. Both approaches fall short: one stalls progress, the other burns energy without results. That's where Tim's story comes in.

Spray and Pray Fails

But action alone isn't always enough. Tim, a recent computer science graduate, jumped into overdrive. Determined to break into software engineering, he applied to over one hundred roles in two weeks. His philosophy was simple: volume would solve the problem.

The result was silence—no interviews, no traction.

Weeks went by with no interviews. Tim was taking action—but without calibration. His résumé was generic. His applications were untailored. His networking was nonexistent. Energy was high. Strategy was absent.

The lesson: more activity doesn't create results—better strategy does.

When Tim slowed down and applied the MVP Framework, he recalibrated. He selected three target companies aligned with his skills. He sought feedback from a mentor on his résumé. He began contributing to GitHub projects to demonstrate capability. He reached out to developers within those organizations.

Within weeks, Tim began landing interviews.

Tim's story is the counterpoint of Elena's: doing nothing stalls progress, but doing everything without direction wastes time. The sweet spot is **strategic action**—moving forward with intention, testing, and adjusting as you go. Activity is not the same as progress. Calibration drives conversion.

Together, Elena and Tim show the two extremes: waiting until you're "perfect" versus acting without strategy. The MVP Framework helps you avoid both traps, giving you a middle path that's proactive, focused, and adaptable. With this mindset in place, let's turn to how you can work with this block in your own career.

Working with This Block

Execution requires structure.

Begin by defining one meaningful action you will take this week. Avoid the temptation to overhaul everything at once. Progress builds from small, consistent moves.

Install a feedback loop. Measure conversion rates: applications, outreaches, responses, and conversations. Treat every interaction as data, not judgment.

Adjust quickly. If something is not working after several attempts, refine your inputs. Rapid iteration prevents wasted months.

Repeat and scale. Once you identify what generates traction, expand intentionally.

Strategic action transforms uncertainty into measurable forward motion.

Exercises for You

1. **One Bold Step:** Execute one deliberate action within the next 48 hours (e.g. send one outreach, apply to one role, ask for one referral).

2. **Measure the Data:** Record every action—number of applications, outreaches, responses.

3. **Reflection Loop:** After each interaction, document one lesson learned. What worked? What didn't?

4. **Weekly Review:** Adjust and refine strategy and set new actions every seven days.

5. **Amplify Traction:** Identify one action producing the strongest return and double it next week.

Closing Reflection

Inaction preserves uncertainty. Execution resolves it.

You don't think your way into clarity—you act your way into it. By applying the *MVP Framework for Career Actions,* you learn by doing. Each deliberate step—however small—reduces ambiguity and increases direction.

When action becomes structured and iterative, progress becomes less random and more predictable. Clarity without action is stagnation.

Write this on a sticky note:

Place it where you plan your week. Let it remind you that forward movement, not flawless planning, builds careers.

The CEO-Mindset

- **Execution determines outcome.** CEOs don't get credit for plans—they get credit for results. Apply the same standard to your career.

- **Test before perfecting.** Launch small actions first, collect feedback, and refine as you go.

- **Track and measure.** Just like CEOs study dashboards, monitor your outreach, applications, and responses to guide strategy.

- **Double down on traction.** Once you see what works, invest more energy there instead of scattering effort everywhere.

Transition to Support Channels

You now have rhythm. You have momentum.

But sustained execution is rarely a solo endeavor.

The next question becomes: Who is reinforcing your discipline and expanding your reach?

In the next chapter, we formalize your Support Channels—the mentors, peers, and allies who strengthen accountability and widen opportunity.

12

CHAPTER

SUPPORT CHANNELS

Careers are often described as personal journeys. In reality, they are collective efforts. No one builds anything meaningful alone—not a company, not a movement, not a lasting career. Behind every visible success is an invisible network of people who advised, challenged, encouraged, and opened doors at critical moments. Your network is not a safety net—it's a force multiplier.

At this stage, you have clarified your direction, defined your value, mapped your resources, and begun executing with intention. But here is the truth that separates sustained growth from short bursts of progress: momentum is easier to start than it is to maintain. Sustained growth requires support.

That's why Block 9 of the *Bullish Career Canvas* asks: *Who can offer me guidance and support?* In other words, Who's in your corner? Who reinforces your ambition when energy dips? Who sharpens your thinking when you drift? Who speaks your name when you are not in the room?

Think of Block 9 like professional racing. Even the most talented driver does not win without a pit crew. Behind every lap are mechanics, strategists, and engineers who refuel, recalibrate, and protect performance under pressure. The driver may get the spotlight, but the crew makes the speed sustainable. Careers work the same way. You are the driver—but your mentors, peers, sponsors, and communities are the crew that keep you competitive (see **Figure 12.1**).

CHALLENGES What's blocking my progress right now?	DESIRED ROLE(S) What job roles or functions am I aiming for?	TARGETED COMPANIES + SECTORS What industries or employers am I focusing on?	SKILL/EXPERIENCE GAPS What am I missing today?	STRATEGIC ACTIONS What steps will I take now?
	UNIQUE VALUE PROPOSITION + THE PITCH What's my personal "wow" factor?	ESSENTIAL SKILLS + CAREER VALUES What skills (hard & soft) are required for these roles?	AVAILABLE RESOURCES What resources can I leverage to advance my career?	SUPPORT CHANNELS Who can offer me guidance and support? **9**
SUCCESS INDICATORS What does success look like?	KEY METRICS How will I measure my progress?		CONTINUOUS LEARNING How will I keep expanding my knowledge and skills?	

Figure 12.1: Block 9—Support Channels

Why This Block Matters

Support channels do not replace effort. They amplify it.

Alone, you can make progress. With the right people behind you, you accelerate. Here's why they matter:

- **Perspective**: Mentors and peers can see blind spots you can't. They notice patterns in your behavior, strengths in your work, and gaps in your thinking.

- **Accountability**: When you say your goals out loud, they become real. When someone asks about them next week, they become urgent.

- **Opportunities**: Referrals and introductions often come from ties in your network—the person you met once, the alum you followed up with, the former manager who remembers your work ethic.

- **Resilience**: When rejection emails pile up or confidence dips, encouragement from others keeps you steady.

Without a pit crew, burnout becomes likely. With one, progress becomes sustainable.

But support is not accidental. It requires structure.

The Career Pit Crew

The pit crew metaphor is not just illustrative—it is instructive.

In racing, pit stops are choreographed to the second. Each member has a defined responsibility. There is no confusion about who changes the tires or who manages fuel. There is no ego competing for attention. There is execution.

Your career deserves the same intentional design.

- **Mentors**: They serve as your crew chief. They zoom out and help you see the broader terrain. They prevent small mistakes from becoming expensive detours.

- **Sponsors**: They are insiders with influence. They advocate for you in rooms you have not yet entered. They convert performance into visibility.

- **Peers**: They run alongside you. They share insights, exchange opportunities, and remind you that growth is rarely linear.

- **Communities**: They expand your ecosystem. Alumni networks, associations, and professional groups increase exposure and belonging.

- **Specialists**: They are recruiters, career coaches, advisors—fine-tune your positioning when precision matters most.

You are the driver, but your progress depends on the coordinated support of these roles. When these roles are defined, your career stops feeling reactive. It becomes supported, calibrated, and sustainable (see **Figure 12.2**).

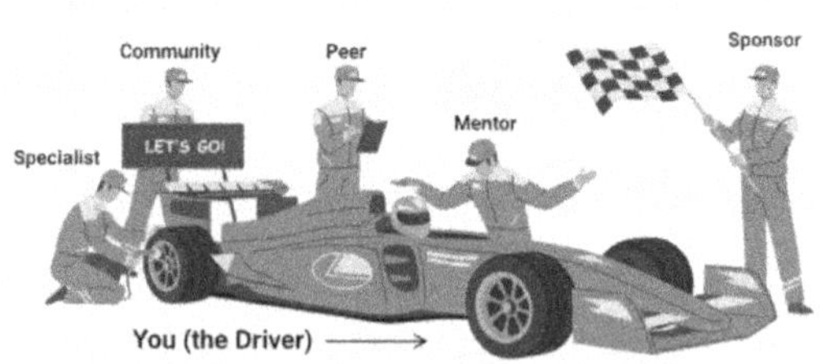

Figure 12.2: The Career Pit Crew

Pit Crew Standard for Job Seekers

Borrowing from the high-performance world of racing, a pit crew is not casual support. It is coordinated precision under pressure. When your career support system is functioning at its best, it operates with the same intentional discipline.

Here's what that standard looks like:

1. **Working in unison**: Everyone understands their lane. Advice doesn't conflict; it complements. Conversations reinforce direction rather than dilute it.

2. **Clear feedback loops**: You update them. They respond. Adjustments happen quickly. Momentum is protected.

3. **Shared purpose**: They genuinely want to see you succeed, not just "grab coffee." They are invested in your growth.

4. **Defined roles**: One helps refine your résumé. Another opens referral doors. Another challenges your thinking before interviews. Clarity prevents overreliance on a single relationship.

5. **No ego**: No one competes for influence in your life. There is collaboration, not control. The goal is your advancement—not their validation.

6. **Bias for action**: Feedback leads to movement. Advice translates into execution. Conversations produce next steps.

7. **Fix what's urgent**: Like a pit stop, attention goes to what moves the needle now—not theoretical perfection months away.

8. **Right tools**: Templates, introductions, mock interviews, insight into hiring patterns—practical support replaces vague encouragement.

9. **Continuous refinement**: Every conversation sharpens your thinking. Every interaction strengthens your positioning.

When your pit crew meets this standard, your career does not drift. It accelerates with discipline.

But speed alone is not enough. Speed without coverage creates vulnerability. That is where the Circle of Support strengthens the model.

The Circle of Support

If the pit crew represents performance under pressure, the *Circle of Support* represents breadth and stability. Together, they form a dual lens: one ensures execution, the other ensures sustainability.

A healthy circle includes:

- **Mentors**: experienced guides who've walked the path before you.

- **Sponsors**: influential allies who advocate for you when you're not in the room.

- **Peers**: colleagues or classmates who provide shared experiences, honest feedback, and mutual accountability.

- **Communities**: alumni groups, professional associations, and industry networks that expand your reach beyond your immediate environment.

Together, they create a layered ecosystem: people who guide strategically, people who challenge you tactically, people who open doors structurally, and people who remind you emotionally that setbacks are temporary.

Organizations understand this principle deeply—which is why many invest in roles dedicated to building community.

Inside Look — The Marketing Community Manager

Many companies hire Marketing Community Managers for one reason: community multiplies performance.

Their role is to cultivate conversations, connect members, highlight success stories, and create environments where customers support one another. They moderate, encourage, and expand the network so value compounds beyond the company itself.

In essence, they build and manage the company's pit crew.

For your career, the same principle applies. You are both the brand and the community manager. It is your responsibility to identify the people who fuel your growth, nurture those relationships intentionally, and maintain engagement over time.

If organizations dedicate full-time roles to building ecosystems of support, why would you leave your own support system to chance?

Support is not a luxury. It is infrastructure.

Your Pit Crew Makes You Go

Take Nina, an early-career UX designer. She often set learning goals but found herself slipping when work deadlines picked up. That changed when she joined a small accountability group with three other designers she met through a Slack community. Every Friday, they shared progress and challenges.

- One week, Nina admitted she hadn't practiced her design challenge exercises.

- Another member suggested a new mock-interview site and offered to pair up.

- Over time, they traded referrals, job postings, and even practiced presentations together.

The lesson: progress accelerates when accountability is shared.

What made this group so powerful was that, without even planning it, they operated like a pit crew:

- One peer stepped into the **mentor role**, providing tough but constructive feedback.

- Another acted as a **specialist**, directing her the mock-interview tools.

- The group became her **community**, celebrating wins and maintaining momentum when energy dipped.

The group wasn't fancy—no coaches, no fees, no structure. But the consistency of weekly check-ins kept Nina on track.

Within six months, Nina's confidence strengthened. When a referral came through from a group member, she was ready.

Nina's breakthrough wasn't a single course or credential. It was support turned into system.

Support is not about prestige—it's about reliability.

How to Work with This Block

1. **Map Your Pit Crew**: Write down who's advising, sponsoring, challenging, and encouraging you today. Where are the gaps?

2. **Diversify the Roles**: Don't lean on one person for everything. Spread support across mentors, peers, and communities.

3. **Give Before You Ask**: Strong channels are built on reciprocity. Share resources, feedback, or encouragement first.

4. **Stay Consistent**: Whether it's monthly mentor calls or weekly peer check-ins, rhythm creates momentum.

5. **Evaluate Your Crew**: Every 6–12 months, ask: are these relationships still helping me grow? Adjust as needed.

Exercises for You

1. **Pit Crew Map**: Draw a circle and list the names of mentors, sponsors, peers, and communities in each quadrant.

2. **One Outreach**: Identify one gap in your circle and commit to reaching out to someone new this month.

3. **Reciprocity Check**: For each relationship, ask: how can I give back?

4. **Community Scan**: Research one new community (online group, association, or alumni network) to join.

5. **Accountability Partner**: Choose one peer to check in with regularly on progress.

Closing Reflection

Your career is not a solo race. It's a coordinated effort, powered by the people who guide, challenge, and champion you along the way.

The *Career Pit Crew* keeps you agile and focused, while the *Circle of Support* keeps you balanced and sustained. Together, they remind you that lasting performance isn't just about skill. It's structure—the invisible network behind every visible win.

Write this on a sticky note:

Place it where you plan your week—a reminder that you don't have to do this alone.

The CEO-Mindset

- **No CEO goes it alone.** Behind every leader is a board, advisors, and advocates. Build yours intentionally.

- **Define the roles.** Pit crews don't guess who does what—neither should you. Assign mentors, peers, and communities clear places in your support system.

- **Create accountability.** Share your goals with your pit crew so they can help you stay aligned.

> **Invest in relationships early.** Communities and allies are long-term assets. Nurture them before you need them, and they'll multiply your opportunities when it counts.

Transition to Career Community

Your pit crew keeps you fueled and focused. But there's one more layer - support grows from one-to-one relationships into something larger—a living ecosystem that expands opportunity beyond your immediate circle.

In the next chapter, we'll explore how to build not just support channels, but a Career Community—an environment where growth becomes sustainable and self-reinforcing.

13

CHAPTER

YOUR CAREER COMMUNITY

Before we move on to the next block of the *Bullish Career Canvas*, let's pause for a moment. You have clarified your direction. You have defined your value. You have mapped your gaps, activated your resources, and assembled your pit crew. You are no longer drifting— you are building. But here's the truth—no meaningful career is built in isolation.

The next level many job seekers overlook is this shift: moving beyond one-to-one relationships and into something far more powerful—a living career community.

A network is a list of contacts. A community is a living system— people who learn together, solve together, and vouch for one another.

Brands understand this deeply. They do not just collect customers; they cultivate communities. Because loyalty compounds when people feel connected—not just to the brand, but to each other. The same principle governs careers: Networks connect you; communities compound you.

That is why community deserves its own chapter. Support channels give you individual allies. A career community creates a one-to-many ecosystem that sustains you long after a single job search ends.

Network vs. Community (and Why It Matters)

The distinction is subtle but important.

A network is transactional. It answers the question: *Who do I know?*

A community is transformational. It answers the question: *Who grows with me?*

It's the shift from collecting contacts to cultivating relationships. It's about engaging consistently and creating a thriving, supportive space around your work.

- In a network, you exchange business cards.
- In a community, you exchange perspective, ideas, encouragement, advice, and opportunity.

Networks fade if left untended; communities thrive when nurtured.

A well-tended career community insulates you during slow markets. It keeps you visible when hiring cools. It creates serendipity when opportunity shifts. It becomes the difference between searching alone and moving with collective momentum.

For job seekers, this requires a mindset shift. You are no longer passively expanding contacts. You are actively cultivating an ecosystem. You share insight. You introduce others. You ask thoughtful questions. You contribute before you need something.

Your job search stops being transactional. It becomes relational. And over time, relationships compound in ways résumés never can.

Four Pillars of a Career Community

Strong communities are not accidents. They are designed.

Think of your career community like a tree. What you see above the surface—referrals, interviews, collaborations—are the branches. But what sustains it are the roots.

As shown in **Figure 13.1**, your *Career Community* rests on four roots.

1. **Content — Show What You're About**

   Share concise, useful content that signals your skills, interests, and values.

   - Student: "3 takeaways from volunteering at the campus analytics lab."

   - Recent Grad: A 10-slide teardown of three job postings → skills map → how you upskilled.

- Early Professional: A one-pager on how you automated a weekly report (before/after impact). *Cadence: 1 short post every 1–2 weeks. Clarity over polish.*

2. **Conversation — Talk With, Not At**

Communities don't grow where monologues dominate. They grow where dialogue lives. Respond with curiosity, ask thoughtful questions, and contribute regularly.

Habit: 10 minutes, 3 thoughtful comments, 5 days a week.

3. **Connection — Be the Bridge**

Introduce people intentionally ("you two should meet because…"). When you connect others, something subtle happens. You become a trusted node in the network— someone who adds value beyond your own needs.

Rule: 1 warm intro per week.

4. **Co-Creation — Build Together**

Shared projects create shared stakes. Co-host a micro-panel, co-write a short guide, or run mock interview sessions. When people build with you, they root for you and rooting leads to referrals.

Experiment: A monthly 20-minute micro-panel with 3 peers on Zoom.

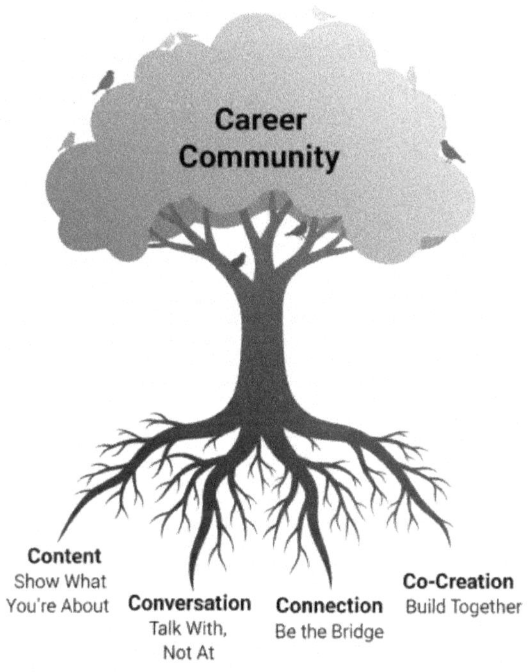

Figure 13.1: The Four Pillars of a Career Community

A career community grows like a tree. Content, Conversation, Connection, and Co-Creation are the roots that feed and sustain it. The stronger the roots, the more durable your community becomes. Careers accelerate whey you are known, and they endure when you are known well.

The Quiet Builder

When Mateo graduated with a degree in mechanical engineering, he believed what most high-performing students believe: if his résumé was strong enough, the right opportunity would find him. He had solid grades, a respected internship, and technical skills that translated well on his résumé. He applied broadly, tailoring where he could and waiting for momentum to build.

It didn't.

The interviews were occasional. The rejections were polite. The silence between applications grew heavier. Mateo assumed he needed more—another certification, another project, another technical edge to make himself competitive.

But what he was missing wasn't technical—it was relational.

It was community.

During a conversation with a former classmate who had just joined a robotics startup, Mateo noticed something different. His classmate hadn't simply applied to jobs — he had been contributing to engineering forums, engaging in design discussions, attending small meetups, and collaborating on open-source projects. People recognized his name before they ever saw his résumé.

That insight shifted Mateo's strategy.

The lesson: visibility follows contribution—not self-promotion.

He began sharing short reflections on design trade-offs from a personal project he was building. Nothing flashy—just thoughtful breakdowns of mechanical decisions and lessons learned. He engaged in robotics Slack groups, not to promote himself, but to contribute meaningfully. When he noticed engineers discussing similar problems in different threads, he introduced them. When a former classmate struggled with CAD optimization, he offered feedback.

Over time, something began to shift.

Mateo's posts sparked discussion. Engineers began tagging him in conversations. A small group of early-career engineers started meeting monthly to review projects and prepare for interviews. They challenged one another, shared resources, and held each other accountable.

Six months later, one of those engineers forwarded Mateo's name to a hiring manager at a robotics firm before the role was even posted publicly. The manager had already seen Mateo's commentary online and appreciated how he approached problems. The interview felt less like an introduction and more like a continuation of a conversation.

When the offer came, it wasn't just a job—it was validation. It was confirmation that visibility built through contribution travels further than credentials alone.

Mateo hadn't gamed the system—he had integrated into it.

His intelligence hadn't changed. His résumé hadn't dramatically expanded. What changed was his visibility within a community that valued his thinking.

He stopped asking, "How do I get noticed?"

He started asking, "How do I contribute?"

Contribution built trust. Trust built access. Access built opportunity.

That is the power of community.

The following section shows a breakdown of how an effective job seeker may spend their time building their career community. This may vary from person to person, but the focus is on tasks related to content, engagement, and self-brand monitoring.

Building Daily Habits (Your Community Calendar)

For many students, recent graduates, or even early-career professionals, the idea of community-building can feel abstract. That's why it helps to break it down into daily habits. Communities don't grow overnight; they grow from small, repeated actions.

Here's a **Career Community Daily Rhythm**—lightweight, practical, and sustainable:

Morning (15–20 minutes)

- Scan your feed
- Comment thoughtfully on 2–3 posts.
- Share one quick insight or takeaway (e.g. article, takeaway, or resource).

Afternoon (10–15 minutes)

- Send one intentional outreach (e.g. alumni, peer, or mentor) with a specific question or note.

- Introduce two people in your network who should connect.

Evening (10 minutes)

- Reflect: Did you add value today?

- Draft a note for tomorrow's post or comment.

This rhythm compounds quietly. In a week, you've touched dozens of people, shared visible insights, and built equity with your community. In a month, you've built visibility. In a quarter, you've created momentum that compounds into referrals, collaborations, and opportunities.

Designing Probability

Irene, an early-career professional, was recently laid off from her first job after college. She was anxious to get back on the job hunt. With only 200 LinkedIn connections and no interviews, she knew she needed to change her approach.

After working through career coaching sessions, she decided to build her community intentionally.

The lesson: community can be built deliberately—not left to chance.

- **Content**: Weekly "feature breakdowns" of popular apps (10-slide carousels).

- **Conversation**: Thoughtful comments on PM and analytics leaders' posts.
- **Connection**: Introduced classmates to a startup founder she met at a meetup.
- **Co-Creation**: Co-hosted a 25-minute "SQL for PMs" micro-workshop with a peer.

Results (6 weeks): 4 warm intros, 3 recruiter screens, 2 panel invites, 1 job offer.

This wasn't luck—it was designed.

Irene's community didn't just support her—it created opportunities.

Irene's story highlights the difference between waiting for luck and designing a system where opportunity comes looking for you. That's the power of community. It changes the probability of success.

Creating a Community Calendar

Building community can feel messy if you don't bring structure to it. That's where a simple community calendar comes in—not as a burden, but as a system that keeps you visible and consistent. Structure prevents burnout.

Here are a few best practices:

- **Start small**: Don't overcomplicate. A simple spreadsheet or notebook can track posts, comments, and outreach.

- **Use filters and themes**: Group activities by the four pillars (e.g. Content, Conversation, Connection, Co-Creation).

- **Balance cadence with capacity**: Better to post once a week consistently than daily for two weeks and then stop.

- **Align with goals**: Need interviews? Focus on conversations and connections. Need visibility? Lean into content.

- **Evaluate monthly**: Check what activities led to engagement, intros, or opportunities. Double down on what's working.

Community building is not about volume. It's about rhythm.

Exercises for You

1. **Define Your Topic Lanes**: Choose 2–3 themes you can speak about consistently.

2. **Design Your First Sprint**: Commit to a 30–30–30 challenge (e.g. 30 comments, 30 new connections, 30 quick conversations in 30 days).

3. **Draft One Co-Creation Invite**: Ask a peer to join you in a low-stakes collaboration (mini-session, guide, or panel).

4. **Map Your Rings**: Identify your Inner Circle (5–7 advisors), Active Circle (~25 peers), and Ambient Circle (100+ light-touch connections).

5. **Measure Engagement**: Track DMs, introductions, screens, referrals.

Closing Reflection

A career community isn't about vanity metrics—it's about resilience, visibility, and belonging. When markets tighten, communities protect you. When opportunities arise, communities amplify you.

Think of your career community as a living system. Tend the roots—content, conversation, connection, and co-creation—and the branches above will flourish.

You won't just be job searching. You'll be ecosystem building that continues working for you after a single opportunity closes.

Write this on a sticky note:

Place it where you'll see it before networking events—a reminder that relationships always come before results.

The CEO-Mindset

- **Communities compound.** The most durable companies in the world are built on loyal ecosystems, not one-time transactions. Build your career the same way.

- **Networks connect; communities sustain.** A contact may give you a lead; a community keeps you relevant when markets shift.

- **Show up consistently.** CEOs don't advertise once and stop. Visibility grows through regular posts, comments, and conversations.

- **Create value before you need it.** Communities thrive on generosity. Share, connect, and co-create before asking for help.

Transition to Evidence

Individual allies and thriving communities give you strength. But one final question remains: *How do you know if all this effort is working?*

In **Part IV — EVIDENCE**, we move from momentum to measurement. Clarity, community, and execution are powerful. But without proof, they remain belief instead of evidence.

Next, we define the Success Indicators that transform your progress into data.

PART FOUR

EVIDENCE

14

CHAPTER

———

SUCCESS INDICATORS

When job seekers are asked, *What does success look like for you?"* the answers are almost always the same:

- *"When I finally land a job."*
- *"Once I sign an offer letter."*
- *"As soon as I get my first paycheck."*

Those are meaningful milestones. But if the only definition of success you hold is the final offer, you will miss dozens of victories along the way—and the confidence that comes with recognizing them. Worse, you will misinterpret silence as stagnation, when progress may already be unfolding beneath the surface.

Success is not a single event. It is a pattern of evidence. Evidence is what separates intention from credibility.

Why This Block Matters

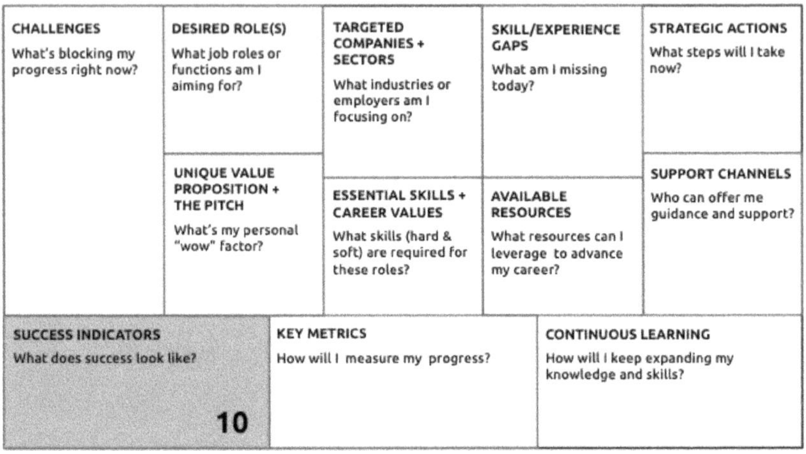

CHALLENGES What's blocking my progress right now?	DESIRED ROLE(S) What job roles or functions am I aiming for?	TARGETED COMPANIES + SECTORS What industries or employers am I focusing on?	SKILL/EXPERIENCE GAPS What am I missing today?	STRATEGIC ACTIONS What steps will I take now?
	UNIQUE VALUE PROPOSITION + THE PITCH What's my personal "wow" factor?	ESSENTIAL SKILLS + CAREER VALUES What skills (hard & soft) are required for these roles?	AVAILABLE RESOURCES What resources can I leverage to advance my career?	SUPPORT CHANNELS Who can offer me guidance and support?

SUCCESS INDICATORS What does success look like? **10**	KEY METRICS How will I measure my progress?	CONTINUOUS LEARNING How will I keep expanding my knowledge and skills?

Figure 14.1: Block 10—Success Indicators

In business, no leader launches a strategy without defining *success indicators* (see **Figure 14.1**). Companies establish KPIs before the quarter begins. Entrepreneurs track customer acquisition before profitability. Project managers measure milestones long before completion.

Yet job seekers—both college students and seasoned professionals—rarely adopt this discipline. *Why not?*

Your career deserves a scoreboard too.

Success indicators turn the invisible grind of applications and outreach into visible progress—proof you can track, celebrate, and build on.

Just as CEOs measure revenue trends before earnings are reported, you need leading indicators that signal traction before the offer letter arrives. When you define success properly, you stop waiting to feel successful—you begin recognizing that you already are building it.

In coaching conversations, when I ask, *"How will you know you're succeeding?"* I often see hesitation. Sometimes discomfort. Most people were taught to chase outcomes, not to measure progress.

This is where many job seekers get stuck—not because they lack talent, but because they lack definition.

When I designed the *Bullish Career Canvas*, I considered placing this block at the very beginning. But defining success requires perspective. It requires clarity. It requires enough distance from panic to think strategically. That is why it comes here—after you've clarified direction, sharpened your value, built community, and taken action.

You now have enough awareness to define progress intentionally.

And sometimes, you need help seeing it. Mentors, career counselors, and trusted peers often spot wins you overlook— focus gained, confidence strengthened, relationships built. These may not look like offer letters, but they are evidence of readiness.

Guiding Questions

Before you define your own indicators, ask yourself:

- *How will I know I'm moving in the right direction?*

- *Is success only about landing a role, or also about growth and skill expansion?*

- *What small wins could I celebrate this month?*

- *One year from now, what would "career readiness" truly mean in my life?*

Answering these questions brings the framework to life. These questions shift you from vague hope to measurable intention.

The Bullish Success Pyramid

This is where structure help—structure reduces anxiety.

The *Bullish Success Pyramid* simplifies success into three levels (see **Figure 14.2**). Think of it as your personal scorecard—a way to see forward motion even when the final outcome hasn't arrived.

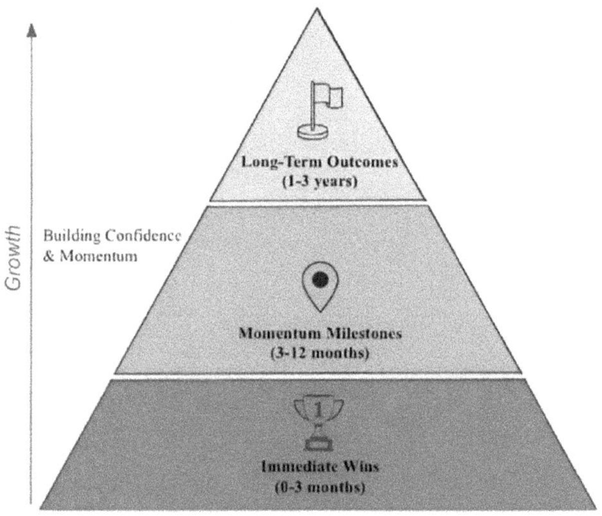

Figure 14.2: Bullish Success Pyramid

Immediate Wins at the base, Momentum Milestones in the middle, and Long-Term Outcomes at the top. Each layer builds confidence for the next.

1. **Immediate Wins (0–3 months):**

   Fast signals that show traction.

   - Recruiter responses

   - Alumni conversations

   - Portfolio updates

   - Informational interviews

   - Improved clarity in your pitch

These are leading indicators. They signal doors are cracking open.

2. **Momentum Milestones (3–12 months):**

   Proof your trajectory is strengthening.

   - Securing an internship or stretch project

   - Completing a certification or workshop

   - Receiving strong interview feedback

   - Growing your professional visibility

   - Leading an initiative

Momentum milestones tell you that your effort is compounding.

3. **Long-Term Outcomes (1–3 years):**

Visible results.

- Landing a full-time role or promotion

- Completing a certification

- Receiving strong interview feedback

- Growing your professional visibility

- Aligning your values with work

The top of the pyramid matters. But it stands only because of the layers beneath it.

Success is not a single moment—it's built layer by layer. Each win, milestone, and outcome is proof that you're moving forward. With the pyramid as your guide, you'll always have evidence of progress—and the momentum to keep climbing.

Wins that Matter

Penny, an economics major, felt stuck because her only definition of success was *"getting a job offer."* Every rejection felt like failure.

We reframed her definition applying the *Bullish Success Pyramid*:

- **Immediate Wins:** Three recruiter replies within sixty days; two portfolio projects published online.

- **Near-Term Milestones:** Secure a summer internship; complete a SQL certificate.

- **Long-Term Outcomes:** Transition into a full-time analyst role with growth potential.

Suddenly, everything shifted. Instead of waiting for the final outcome, Penny began tracking movement.

- Each email reply became proof.
- Each project became progress.
- Each interview became data.

The lesson: what you measure defines how you experience progress.

Within a few months, Penny received two internship offers. But what mattered most was that she stopped feeling stuck long before those offers arrived.

The breakthrough wasn't new talent-it was new definition.

When you redefine success, you reclaim control over your experience of the search.

I share Penny's story because I've seen this play out hundreds of times. The problem usually isn't a lack of talent—it's a lack of definition. When job seekers only celebrate the final outcome, they burn out quickly. But once they define success at different levels, the weight of the job search lifts. They can see movement, even before the offer letter arrives.

That's why this block requires discipline. You're not just reacting to the market—you're building a system for recognizing progress.

Celebrating Wins and Learning from Setbacks

Progress is rarely linear. Success isn't just about the big outcomes. It's also about the *small wins* that prove momentum is real, and the *setbacks* that teach you how to adjust. In one-on-one coaching sessions, I often see job seekers so focused on the end result that they forget the journey. But celebrating small wins along the way keeps you encouraged and focused (see **Figure 14.3**).

Figure 14.3: Growth Through Wins and Setbacks

Celebrate Small Wins

Every recruiter reply, alumni conversation, and portfolio update is progress—not minor steps, but fuel. Taking the time to acknowledge them boosts confidence and keeps motivation alive.

Learn from Setbacks

Not every outreach will get a reply. Not every interview will go well. That's not failure—that's data. CEOs study missed targets to refine strategy; you should do the same. Ask: *What worked? What didn't? What will I do differently next time?*

Embrace the Process

Progress isn't linear. Success indicators remind you that setbacks don't erase momentum. They're part of the climb. Each win and stumble is building resilience, clarity, and growth.

Of course, getting a job offer is a big win. But even if the role isn't your dream job, it's proof that you're valuable in the market. You don't have to accept every offer, but you should celebrate the success of earning one. It validates your effort, skills, and persistence—and it reminds you the right opportunity is out there.

Ways to celebrate your job search milestones

Celebrating doesn't need to be extravagant—it just needs to be intentional:

- **Keep a win journal.** Write down every milestone you hit. Looking back builds confidence on tough days.

- **Share your progress.** Tell friends, family, or mentors. Verbalizing reinforces your wins and inspires others

- **Reward yourself.** A favorite coffee, a short walk, or an episode of Netflix—small treats fuel momentum.

- **Pause mindfully.** Take a breath, reflect, and acknowledge before jumping to the next task.

From Indicators to a Scorecard

Defining success indicators is powerful. Tracking them is transformational. Just as companies use dashboards to measure performance, you can build a **Personal Career Scorecard** (see **Figure 14.4**).

Start simple: list 3–5 success indicators across the three levels of the pyramid. Then check in weekly or monthly: did I see progress? Am I closer to my near-term milestone?

Example (Recent Graduate):

Success Indicator	Type	Timeline	Status
3 recruiter replies	Immediate	60 days	2/3 achieved
SQL Certification	Near-Term	6 months	Enrolled
Full-time role	Long-Term	12 months	In progress

Figure 14.4: Example of Personal Career Scorecard

This isn't about perfection. It's about direction, accountability, and proof. Progress feels slower than it is—numbers prove otherwise. Here's the coaching tip: if you don't measure it, you won't believe it. Success indicators aren't just reflections of effort—they're evidence you can point to when doubt creeps in.

Exercises for You

1. **Draft Your Pyramid:** Define 2–3 indicators for each level: Immediate, Near-Term, Long-Term.

2. **Build Your Scorecard:** Create a simple table or spreadsheet with 3–5 indicators to measure weekly.

3. **Celebrate Small Wins:** Define how you'll acknowledge immediate Wins (e.g. coffee with a mentor, journaling, sharing with a friend).

4. **One-Year Statement:** Write a short reflection: *"One year from now, I'll feel successful if…"*

5. **Share It:** Tell someone who will hold you accountable.

Closing Reflection

If you take nothing else from this chapter, take this: *You need to know what success looks like for you before you chase it.*

Don't outsource that definition to employers, market trends, or luck. Own it. Define it. Write it down. Share it with someone who will hold you accountable. That single act can transform how you experience your job search. Clarity without measurement breeds doubt. But clarity with evidence builds confidence.

Write this on a sticky note:

Place it near your job search tracker. Let it remind you that momentum matters just as much as outcomes.

The CEO-Mindset

- **Define success early.** CEOs never launch without success metrics. Neither should you.

- **Measure leading indicators.** Job offers are lagging results. Celebrate recruiter replies, interviews, and portfolio updates along the way.

- **Celebrate traction.** Success isn't one big leap—it's momentum built step by step.

- **Use a scorecard.** What gets measured gets managed. A personal career scorecard keeps you honest and confident.

Transition to Key Metrics

You now know what success looks like. But defining it isn't enough—you also need to measure it consistently.

In the next chapter, we move to **Block 11:** *Key Metrics*, where you'll turn your success indicators into a weekly scoreboard that strengthens accountability, sharpens strategy, and keeps your momentum measurable. Belief motivates, but evidence is undeniable.

15

CHAPTER

KEY METRICS

Most job seekers confuse activity with progress. They count résumés sent instead of results earned. But let's be clear: résumés sent are not success. They are inputs. Inputs without conversion are noise.

In the previous chapter, you defined your success indicators—the signals that show you're moving in the right direction. But indicators without measurement are just intention. This is where many searches stall. People work hard, but they don't' know whether their effort is working.

That's why Block 11 of the *Bullish Career Canvas* focuses on **metrics** (see **Figure 15.1**). Just as companies run on dashboards, scorecards, and KPIs, your career deserves a system that tells you what is gaining traction, what is flat, and what is quietly draining your energy.

Without metrics, you drift in "job search fog"—sending out applications, scrolling job boards, and hoping something sticks, without knowing what's actually working. With metrics, you operate with focus.

Why This Block Matters

CHALLENGES	DESIRED ROLE(S)	TARGETED COMPANIES + SECTORS	SKILL/EXPERIENCE GAPS	STRATEGIC ACTIONS
What's blocking my progress right now?	What job roles or functions am I aiming for?	What industries or employers am I focusing on?	What am I missing today?	What steps will I take now?

UNIQUE VALUE PROPOSITION + THE PITCH	ESSENTIAL SKILLS + CAREER VALUES	AVAILABLE RESOURCES	SUPPORT CHANNELS
What's my personal "wow" factor?	What skills (hard & soft) are required for these roles?	What resources can I leverage to advance my career?	Who can offer me guidance and support?

SUCCESS INDICATORS	KEY METRICS	CONTINUOUS LEARNING
What does success look like?	How will I measure my progress?	How will I keep expanding my knowledge and skills?

Figure 15.1: Block 11—Key Metrics

CEOs do not run companies on vibes. They run on data.

When I ask job seekers how many applications they've submitted, I usually hear: *"a lot."* But "a lot" isn't a number. And if you can't measure it, you can't manage it.

Think about it:

- Athletes track times, reps, and performance.

- Businesses measure revenue, customers, and goals.

- Project managers track milestones, deadlines, and deliverables.

Measurement creates accountability and accountability creates improvement. *Why should your career be any different?*

Metrics strip away illusion. They tell you:

- Is your résumé converting?

- Is your outreach resonating?

- Are interviews progressing?

- Is your strategy compounding—or stalling?

You do not need complexity. In fact, complexity becomes avoidance. The goal is simple: choose a few meaningful metrics, track them consistently, and let the numbers guide your weekly adjustments.

Focus beats perfection.

The Bullish Career Scorecard

Here are five simple metrics you can use to measure progress. You don't need all of them—start with three to five that fit your situation and build from there. If you only measure résumés sent, you'll drown in activity and miss the signals that matter. Instead, start with three to five metrics that reveal conversion—the points where effort becomes outcome.

Here are five core metrics that work across most job searches.

1. **Applications Sent → Interview Rate**

This measures conversion. If you submit 40 applications and receive two interviews, your conversion rate is 5%. That number tells a story.

Low rate? Likely one of three issues:

- Targeting is too broad.
- Résumé isn't translating value.
- Role level is misaligned.

The metric doesn't judge. It diagnoses.

2. Time-to-First-Interview

This measures early traction. If weeks pass without interviews, do not "grind harder." Adjust sooner.

Time is feedback.

3. Outreach → Response Rate

If you send 20 networking messages and receive 2 replies, your response rate is 10%. That is not failure. It is insight.

Low response rate often means:

- Messaging is generic.
- Outreach is too long.
- The reason for reaching out isn't specific.

Personalization improves numbers.

4. Interviews → Offers Ratio

This is one of the most honest metrics you will track. If interviews aren't converting, the issue is not volume—it is positioning, storytelling, focus, or role fit.

When numbers speak, listen.

5. **Momentum Metrics**

These are weekly activity drivers: outreaches sent, follow-ups completed, portfolio artifacts shipped.

Momentum metrics protect you emotionally during quiet weeks. They ensure you are building even when outcomes lag.

A Balanced Approach

In business, leaders often use a **Balanced Scorecard** so they do not over-focus on one dimension. Instead of only tracking financials, they evaluate performance across four perspectives: financial, customer, internal process, and people/staff.

You can apply the same principle to your career. A career scorecard should also be balanced across four dimensions:

- **Opportunities:** Are you generating interviews and offers?
- **Connections:** Are you strengthening the network that creates leverage?
- **Process:** Are your applications and outreach efficient and targeted?
- **Growth:** Are you improving your skills and sharpening your pitch?

If you only apply, you may feel busy but remain invisible. If you only network, you may feel visible but lack conversion. Balance creates leverage.

Keep your career scorecard simple. The right few metrics beat tracking everything.

The Career Readiness Quadrant

Businesses have long used frameworks like the **Gartner Magic Quadrant™** to evaluate market players.

Borrowing from this strategic evaluation model, the *Career Readiness Quadrant* (see **Figure 15.2**) is a simple way to see your position in the job market and, more importantly, how to move forward.

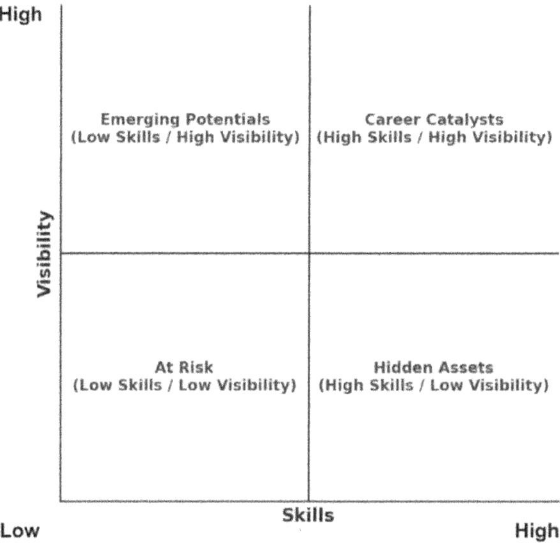

Figure 15.2: Anatomy of the Career Readiness Quadrant

This model uses two dimensions that matter most for job seekers.

- **Skills**: Do you have the capabilities employers need today?
- **Visibility**: Does the market see and recognize your value?

This framework plots **Skills** (horizontal axis) against **Visibility** (vertical axis) to show where job seekers stand in the market. The goal is movement toward the top right—where skills and visibility combine into momentum

1. **Career Catalysts (High Skills / High Visibility)**

   Career Catalysts are capable and recognized. They've built in-demand skills, and they know how to communicate them through networking, personal branding, and interviews.

   Coaching takeaway: If you're here, don't get complacent. Keep stacking skills and expanding visibility so you stay ahead of market shifts.

2. **Hidden Assets (High Skills / Low Visibility)**

   Hidden Assets are strong—but overlooked. They've developed real capability, yet the market can't see it. Their résumé undersells them, their LinkedIn presence is thin, or their networking is inconsistent.

   Coaching takeaway: Your next move isn't more skills—it's visibility. Showcase your work, expand your network, and strengthen your story.

3. **Emerging Potentials (Low Skills / High Visibility)**

Emerging Potentials are visible—they network, they engage, they show up—but their skills haven't caught up yet. Employers may see promise but hesitate without proof.

Coaching takeaway: Visibility is working, but you need skill stacking. Focus on learning, certifications, and practice projects that turn potential into performance.

4. **At Risk (Low Skills / Low Visibility)**

This quadrant feels heavy—because it is. Job seekers here often feel invisible and frustrated.

Coaching takeaway: Don't panic. Everyone starts somewhere. The key is to pick one quick skill to build (i.e. a course, a project, a tool) while taking one small visibility step (update your LinkedIn, attend an event, or post about your learning). Progress in either direction will begin to shift you upward or outward.

The *Career Readiness Quadrant* is not a label—it's a map. It shows where you are today. It also shows you where to move next.

Making the Strategy Real

Ryan, a marketing manager with ten years experience, was a classic *Hidden Asset—high capability, low visibility.* His skills were strong. His visibility was weak. His résumé read like responsibilities—not impact. His outreach was broad and untracked.

On paper, Ryan was qualified. In practice, he was invisible.

We built a simple scorecard:

- Application-to-Interview Rate
- Outreach Response Rate
- Weekly Networking Touchpoints

The lesson: what gets measured gets improved.

Within two weeks, the data exposed blind spots. His messaging was generic. His résumé lacked specificity. His targeting was unfocused.

He adjusted quickly.

He tailored his résumé.

He personalized outreach.

He shared short, thoughtful marketing insights on LinkedIn.

Ryan's response rate rose to 25%. By month's end, he had three interviews scheduled.

Ryan didn't suddenly become more talented. He became more visible—and more strategic.

That's the power of metrics paired with the quadrant: metrics show what's broken; the quadrant explains why.

From Metrics to Momentum

Metrics don't just measure progress—they guide transformation. Numbers reveal patterns, patters reveal leverage, and leverage reveals where to double down. The quadrant shows you the "where," while your scorecard shows you the "how."

Metrics are only powerful if you put them into practice. Numbers by themselves don't create change—but when tracked consistently, they reveal patterns, highlight gaps, and point you toward better strategies.

Leaders in business know this well: they align teams around one growth story, adapt as capability needs evolve, and keep asking the same core question: *"How will this action help us grow?"*

For your career, it's no different. Your résumé, LinkedIn profile, and networking conversations must tell one aligned story. Your metrics should reveal when it's time to update your skills or reframe your pitch. And the CEO question for You, Inc. is simple: *"Does this activity move me closer to my next role?"*

Don't do this in isolation. Share your scorecard with a mentor, career coach, or trusted peer. A second set of eyes can spot progress and blind spots you'll miss when you're too close to the work.

Instead of trying to measure everything, the goal is to identify the few metrics that truly matter, monitor them regularly, and let them guide your adjustments. This is where job seekers shift from "activity" to "momentum."

10 Common Mistakes That Sink Job Searches (and How to Avoid Them)

Most job seekers fall into predictable traps when they try to measure progress. Here are ten mistakes I see repeatedly—and the fixes that may help:

1. **Tracking Nothing**

   - Mistake: Guessing progress based on feelings.

   - Fix: Use a simple scorecard to see facts, not vibes.

2. **Tracking Too Much**

   - Mistake: Measuring everything and improving nothing.

   - Fix: Focus on 3–5 metrics that matter most.

3. **Only Counting Applications**

   - Mistake: Treating "jobs applied" as the main KPI.

   - Fix: Balance with outreach, interviews, and conversions.

4. **Ignoring Response Rates**

   - Mistake: Not noticing silence is a signal.

   - Fix: Track outreach → response and refine your messaging.

5. **Not Measuring Time**

   - Mistake: Missing early warning signs.

- Fix: Track Time-to-First-Interview and time between stages.

6. **Failing to Review Regularly**

- Mistake: Create a scorecard once, then never looking at it again.

- Fix: Review weekly—just like a project check-in.

7. **Measuring Outputs, Not Outcomes**

- Mistake: Counting effort without asking if it converts.

- Fix: Always connect activity to results (apps → interviews → offers).

8. **Not Adjusting When Data Speaks**

- Mistake: Repeating the same approach while results stay flat.

- Fix: Let the numbers force a pivot early.

9. **Comparing to Others' Metrics**

- Mistake: Using someone else's timeline as your scorecard.

- Fix: Track your own progress; careers aren't one-size-fits-all.

10. **Chasing Perfection**

- Mistake: Waiting for flawless tracking before acting.

- Fix: Imperfect tracking beats no tracking—start now.

Exercises for You

1. **Pick Your Metrics:** Choose 3–5 from the list above that fit your job search.

2. **Build Your Scorecard:** Create a simple spreadsheet or notebook page with weekly targets.

3. **Review Weekly:** Ask yourself: What's improving? What's flat? What needs adjusting?

4. **Spot Patterns:** If networking works better than cold applications, shift your energy. If interviews aren't converting, double down on practice and feedback.

Call to Action

Don't just read this chapter—use it. By next week, draft your first version of a scorecard and start tracking at least one metric. The sooner you start, the sooner you'll gain direction.

Closing Reflection

Metrics don't lie. They strip away guesswork, expose patterns, and guide your next move. The sooner you track, the faster you improve. Progress is in the numbers—and the numbers are in your hands.

Write this on a sticky note:

Stick it on your calendar or spreadsheet—a reminder to review your scorecard weekly.

The CEO-Mindset

- **Tell the growth story.** CEOs turn data into narratives that inspire confidence. Treat your career numbers the same way—show progress, not just activity.

- **Focus on meaningful metrics.** Vanity metrics (like résumés sent) don't matter. Measure conversion rates, outreach responses, and actions that drive momentum.

- **Ask the CEO question.** With every action, pause and ask: *"Does this move me closer to growth?"*

- **Adapt fast.** If the data says your approach isn't working, adjust before burnout sets in.

Transition to Continuous Learning

You've now defined success indicators and built a scoreboard of key metrics. But numbers alone aren't enough. The real advantage comes from learning and adapting as you go.

In the next chapter, we'll explore **Block 12**: *Continuous Learning—* how to keep expanding your skills so your progress never stalls.

16

CHAPTER

CONTINUOUS LEARNING

Too many job seekers treat graduation or landing a role as the finish line. But here's the truth: the market doesn't pause because you've got a diploma or a paycheck. Skills expire. Roles evolve. Industries shift. If you're not learning, you're standing still—you're drifting backward while the current moves forward.

In three decades in Silicon Valley, I've seen wave after wave: the rise of the internet, the spread of smartphones, the shift to cloud, the acceleration of AI. Every wave did the same two things at once: it created new roles overnight, and it quietly made older skill sets less valuable. The winners weren't the smartest people in the room. They were the ones who kept learning *before* they were forced to.

Today, cost-cutting and AI adoption are accelerating simultaneously. Entire teams are being restructured in months rather than years. For some, this has meant serial layoffs—multiple job losses within short intervals. For others, it has meant absorbing additional workloads after colleagues were cut. In both cases, exhaustion follows. In Chapter 2, we described this growing strain as *layoff fatigue*—the mental and emotional wear that builds when uncertainty becomes constant. When instability lingers, even high performers begin to question their footing.

Continuous learning is not about panic upskilling. It is about positioning. The professionals who remain steady in volatile markets are rarely the ones scrambling after disruption. They are the ones who built optionality before they needed it.

Why This Block Matters

CHALLENGES What's blocking my progress right now?	DESIRED ROLE(S) What job roles or functions am I aiming for?	TARGETED COMPANIES + SECTORS What industries or employers am I focusing on?	SKILL/EXPERIENCE GAPS What am I missing today?	STRATEGIC ACTIONS What steps will I take now?
	UNIQUE VALUE PROPOSITION + THE PITCH What's my personal "wow" factor?	ESSENTIAL SKILLS + CAREER VALUES What skills (hard & soft) are required for these roles?	AVAILABLE RESOURCES What resources can I leverage to advance my career?	SUPPORT CHANNELS Who can offer me guidance and support?
SUCCESS INDICATORS What does success look like?	KEY METRICS How will I measure my progress?		CONTINUOUS LEARNING How will I keep expanding my knowledge and skills? **12**	

Figure 16.1: Block 12—Continuous Learning

Learning isn't optional anymore—it's the career currency that keeps you employable and future-ready. Employers don't just hire for today's skills; they bet on your ability to keep growing tomorrow. That's why continuous learning is Block 12 of the *Bullish Career Canvas*—it ensures you're always adding fuel to your future (see **Figure 16.1**).

I've met countless professionals who stalled not because they weren't talented, but because they relied on yesterday's strengths. They were excellent at what they did—until what they did stopped being what the market needed. Then the problem wasn't performance. It was *relevance*.

On the other side, I have worked with candidates who immediately stood out because they could say:

> *"I just finished a certification in that area,"*
>
> *"I built a project to learn this skill on my own."*
>
> *"I've been practicing it weekly—and here's what I can show you."*

That language signals more than competence. It signals adaptability, resilience, and drive. Employers cannot teach those qualities—but they recognize them instantly.

Continues learning is not about chasing trends. It is about maintaining relevance.

The Bullish Learning Cadence

Growth does not happen in bursts; it happens in rhythm. If learning only appears when stress spikes—when a layoff hits, when interviews stall, when the market tightens—it becomes reactive and frantic. Panic-learning feels exhausting because it is driven by fear.

The *Bullish Learning Cadence* is different. It's a steady, repeatable actions that builds momentum without burning you out (see **Figure 16.2**). Think of it like training for a long-distance race. You don't cram the night before. You build endurance through consistency.

The cadence has four parts:

1. **Daily Micro-Learning**

    *   15–30 minutes a day.

    *   Articles, podcasts, or short online lessons.

    *   Purpose: stay current and build awareness.

    *   This is your keep the engine warm.

2. **Monthly Practice Projects**

    *   One tangible project a month

    *   A portfolio update, a case study, a write-up/blog post, or presentation.

    *   Purpose: turn knowledge into applied skill.

    *   Knowledge becomes evidence here.

3. **Quarterly Commitments**

    *   A real skill-build every 3-4 months.

    *   A course, certification, stretch assignment or structured learning track.

- Purpose: add a substantial skill to your toolkit.

- This is your level-up cycle.

4. **Annual Growth Goals**

- Define one significant learning milestone each year

- Master a tool, deepen leadership skills, publish a project, present publicly, contribute to a community.

- Purpose: anchor your progress with a milestone that signals growth.

- This is the flag you plant on the mountain.

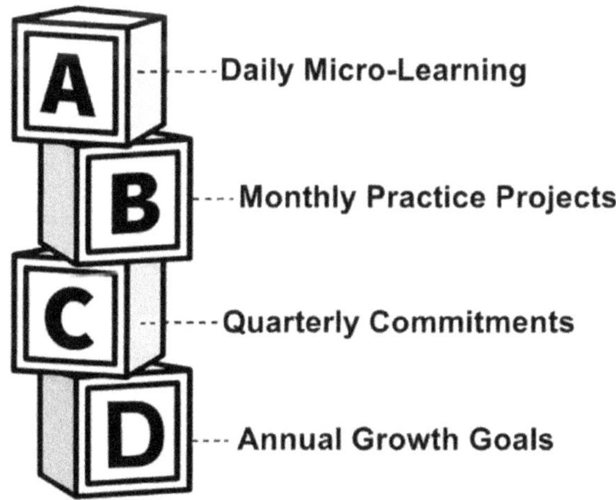

Figure 16.2: The Bullish Learning Cadence

This cadence works because it integrates learning into how you operate. It removes the question of "when will I find time?" and replaces it with "this is simply what I do."

Stackable Skills: The New Career Currency

Think of your skills like building blocks. One block helps. But stacks are what create something real.

A single badge or course is fine—but a stack creates a story. And the real edge today is *hybrid stacks:* technical + human skills combined.

- AI plus communication.

- Data plus leadership.

- Coding plus collaboration.

- Automation plus change management.

Employers increasingly evaluate talent through a skills-first lens. That means your ability to demonstrate capability—through projects, credentials, portfolios, or applied learning—often matters as much as your formal degree or credentials.

A stack tells a story. A single course is an activity. A stack is positioning.

Show, Don't Tell

Kris, a recent graduate, was competing for analyst roles. On paper, she resembled dozens of other candidates—similar GPA, similar coursework, similar internships. But she made one strategic decision: while searching, she committed to building a small portfolio of applied data projects.

When recruiters asked about her skills, Kris did not simply say, *"I know Excel and SQL."* She said, *"I built three dashboards to practice Python and Tableau—I'd love to walk you through them."*

The lesson: demonstrated skills outperform stated skills.

That shift changed the conversation and placed Kris in the top tier of candidates. Instead of defending her qualifications, she demonstrated them. The hiring manager later shared that what stood out was not only her technical ability, but her initiative and enthusiasm every time she walked through her work.

Kris did not just claim growth—she proved it.

The Reality Most People Avoid

Many professionals only prioritize learning after disruption hits. By then, curiosity has turned into urgency. That's when you hear the same lines from talented people who are suddenly back in the market:

> *"I haven't updated my résumé in years."*
>
> *"I don't know how to frame my experience anymore."*
>
> *"I can't even remember the last new skill I added."*

These individuals were not underperforming. They were simply unprepared for change.

Job security is not a tenure. It is not title. It is not even a strong performance review. Job security is relevance—and relevance is built through continuous learning, steady visibility, and proactive career management.

This is not meant to alarm you. It is meant to give you awareness of possibilities. When you build before disruption arrives, you remove panic from the equation. You operate from strength, not fear.

That's why the *Bullish Career Canvas* exists. It's built for everyone: college students, recent graduates, and seasoned professionals alike. It's a system that keeps you building before you need it—so when change comes (and it often will), you're not scrambling from zero.

As CEO of You, Inc., your job security is directly tied to your skill security. That investment cannot be deferred indefinitely.

Barriers to Learning (and How to Beat Them)

The two most common obstacles professionals cite are time and money. The good news—both are manageable when you treat learning like a CEO decision, not a hobby.

- **Time compounds:** Break learning into micro-sessions—Fifteen minutes a day doesn't feel heroic, but it compounds into real hours over a year. It's not about intensity—it's about consistency.

- **Money is rarely the primary constraint:** Free and low-cost platforms, podcasts, and newsletters. Many employers also reimburse education costs as part of their benefit offerings. You'd be surprised how many managers will support growth when you frame it as performance fuel.

- **Access:** You may no longer have a campus library, but you have something better: communities, open-source projects, online cohorts, and people who are learning in public every day.

Time, money, access—they're challenges but not excuses. CEOs don't wait for ideal conditions to invest. They start where they are, with what they have. They allocate resources deliberately.

Exercises for You

1. **Map Your Cadence:** Write down one daily, monthly, quarterly, and annual learning activity.

2. **Apply Immediately:** Choose one skill you're learning and build something with it this month—a project, a write-up, a case study, a portfolio artifact.

3. **Track It:** Add learning milestones to your career scorecard so progress becomes visible.

4. **Share It:** Post one lesson learned on LinkedIn or share it with a mentor. Visibility turns learning into opportunity.

Call to Action

Continuous learning isn't optional anymore—it's your edge. Pick one course, one project, or one book this month. Start now. The market won't wait—and neither should you.

Closing Reflection

Continuous learning is not about chasing every trend. It is about sustaining momentum. Every new skill expands your opportunities. Every applied project strengthens confidence. Every visible artifact builds credibility.

The professionals who thrive long-term are not those who know everything. They are the ones who never stop becoming relevant.

Write this on a sticky note:

Place it near your laptop—Let it remind you to keep investing in your skills daily.

The CEO-Mindset

- **Invest like a CEO.** Treat time and money spent on learning as high-ROI investments.

- **Build your stack.** Stackable skills compound faster than one-off courses.

- **Balance the portfolio.** Hybrid skills (technical + human) make you future-proof.

- **Stay market-ready.** The market shifts fast. Keep your cadence steady so disruption never leaves you behind.

Transition to Next Block

You've now worked through all 12 blocks of the *Bullish Career Canvas*—from defining your challenges to building clarity, community, metrics, and momentum. Each block stands on its own. But together, they form a system—the Bullish Career Loop—a repeatable cycle of Aim, Fit, Action, and Evidence that professionals can use throughout their careers.

In the conclusion – we zoom out and examine how the Career Canvas integrates into a unified blueprint—one you can revisit throughout your career as markets shift, roles evolve, and new waves inevitably arrive. Because careers are not built in a single season. They are built through disciplined cycles of clarity, action, evidence, and growth.

Conclusion

Congratulations. You've done the work. You've walked through all 12 blocks of the *Bullish Career Canvas*—clarifying challenges, defining roles, sharpening your value, mapping resources, and building a rhythm for growth. Each block gave you tools. Together, they form something far more powerful: a system.

At times, the blocks may have felt tactical—a question to answer, a metric to track, a relationship to strengthen. But when you step back, you begin to see the architecture. The canvas is not a worksheet. It is a career operating system—one that runs quietly beneath your decisions and helps you guide updates, pivots, risks, and reinventions long after you close this book.

Think of the *Bullish Career Canvas* as the system running beneath your professional life. It's not a checklist or a template you complete once and forget. Instead, it is a living structure designed to evolve alongside you.

- It fosters collaboration. Share it with a mentor, career counselor, or peer. Let others provide perspective you may not see on your own.

- It drives clarity. Instead of drifting through job boards or second-guessing your résumé, you know where to focus your time and energy.

- It creates momentum. Each block connects to the others, so progress in one area naturally strengthens the others.

Most careers operate without a visible system. People chase titles, respond to postings, and measure progress only by outcomes they cannot fully control. Their résumé is updated only when a crisis forces it. You are no longer drifting—you are operating with a system. You now have structure, language, and visibility into the parts of your career that once felt invisible.

Like any effective leader, you now have a dashboard—challenges named, metrics tracked, resources aligned, and a strategy for growth. This is no longer theory. It is execution.

This is the moment to move from learning to doing. Print your *Bullish Career Canvas*. Sketch it on a whiteboard. Revisit it weekly and refine it monthly. If you are not revisiting your canvas on a regular basis, you are not using it. Let it serve as your north star whenever doubt or distraction appears.

Remember, the *Bullish Career Canvas* is not about perfection; it is about visibility and focus. It illuminates the parts of your career that once felt hidden, helping you see where to act, where to grow, and where to move next.

Traditional tools such as MBTI, DiSC, or StrengthsFinder help you understand who you are. The *Bullish Career Canvas* goes a step further—it helps you decide what to do next. That is why this framework belongs not only in the hands of job seekers, but also career counselors, mentors, and educators. It bridges the gap between self-awareness and strategy, between reflection and action.

Career Flywheel

As your system begins to take shape, something important happens: progress starts to compound. Clarity leads to action. Action produces evidence. Evidence creates signal in the market. And that signal sharpens your clarity again. This is not a linear path—it is a loop (see **Figure C.1**).

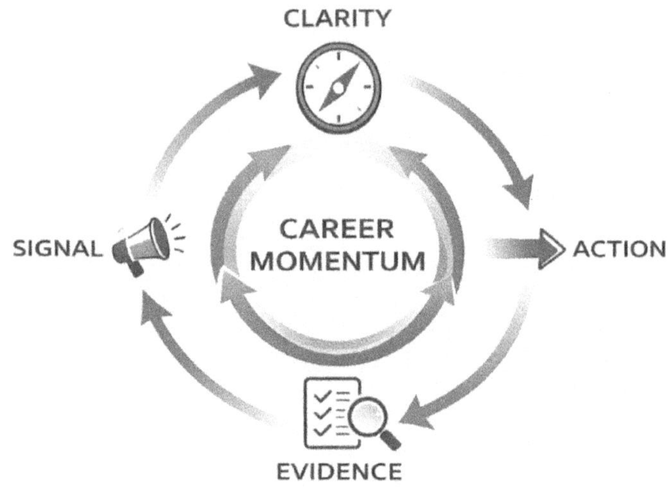

Figure C.1: The Career Flywheel

Think of this as your Career Flywheel—a system where each part of your effort reinforces the next. When you gain clarity, you act with more focus. When you act, you build evidence. When you build evidence, the market responds. And when the market responds, your direction becomes even clearer.

Once this flywheel starts turning, momentum builds. Opportunities become easier to access. Conversations become more meaningful. Your confidence grows—not from guesswork, but from proof.

The goal is not just to move forward. The goal is to create a system where progress feeds itself.

The Sticky Notes Were Never Just Sticky Notes

Throughout this book, you were asked to write things down—on sticky notes, paper, or a whiteboard. At first, it may have felt simple, even elementary: a phrase here, a metric there, a reminder placed near your desk.

But those sticky notes were never just sticky notes.

Designers use sticky notes to break complexity into parts before reconnecting those parts into something meaningful. They spread ideas across a wall so patterns emerge. They make the invisible visible. Without realizing it, you've done the same with your career.

Each note captured something specific—a challenge you named, a role you clarified, a value you sharpened, a gap you committed to closing, a metric you decided to track. Individually, each note seemed small. Together, they became architecture.

That's why the Sticky Board at the end of this book matters. It is not decoration. It's evidence. Evidence that you've moved from vague ambition to structured clarity. Evidence that you've stopped drifting and started designing.

You didn't just complete a framework. You built an operating system. And that's the deeper shift.

The transformation this book was meant to create is not merely tactical—it's psychological. It is the moment you stop waiting to be chosen and start building with intention. It is the realization that your career is not a lottery ticket dependent on timing or luck. It is a system that rewards focus, discipline, and iteration. A system you now know how to maintain, update, and refine.

You are no longer reacting without structure. You are naming your challenges, defining your roles, stacking skills, measuring traction, and learning before disruption forces you to. That is the CEO mindset applied to You, Inc.

And CEOs don't drift. They design.

What happens next is simple—but it is not passive. You continue using the system you have built. When markets shift, you revisit your challenges. When interests evolve, you redefine your roles. When your skills grow, you refine your value proposition. When metrics stall, you adjust your strategy. And when opportunity appears, you recognize it—because you have been preparing for it all along.

This is not a one-time exercise you complete and forget. It is a discipline. A rhythm. A way of thinking about your career that compounds over time.

Clarity without action fades. But clarity paired with action becomes momentum. Momentum builds confidence. Confidence builds resilience. And resilience, compounded over time, becomes something luminous.

Luminous careers are not accidents. They are constructed—intentionally, repeatedly, and with discipline.

Write this on a sticky note:

Place it somewhere you will see it every day—on your desk, laptop, or mirror—not as decoration, but as reinforcement. Let it remind you that your trajectory is not owned by the market, your manager, or chance. It is shaped by your decisions, your discipline, and your willingness to keep building.

You don't need to have everything figured out. You simply need a system—and the discipline to use it.

Now you have one.

Stay curious, stay accountable, and keep building.

And above all, stay Bullish.

Don't close this book and move on—open your canvas and begin. Because clarity isn't found. It's built—one decision at a time.

APPENDIX

BONUS MATERIAL

Bullish Career Canvas

CHALLENGE(S)

What's blocking your progress right now? (e.g. no clarity, lack of confidence, no experience)

DESIRED ROLE(S)

What job roles or functions are you aiming for?

ESSENTIAL SKILLS + CAREER VALUES

What skills (hard & soft) are required for these roles? What values are important to you in a job for you to thrive?

UNIQUE VALUE PROPOSITION + THE PITCH

What makes you worth hiring? What's your personal "wow" factor? Can you describe your story in 2-3 sentences?

SKILL/EXPERIENCE GAPS

What are you missing today? What's holding you back from being competitive?

STRATEGIC ACTIONS

What steps will you take now? (e.g. Update résumé, network, take a course, etc.)

AVAILABLE RESOURCES

What career center services, courses, professors, platforms, or mentors can you use?

TARGETED COMPANIES/ SECTORS

What industries or employers are you focusing on? Do your skills align with these companies?

SUPPORT CHANNELS

Who can offer guidance and support? (e.g. Alumni, advisors, professors, former coworkers, friends, etc.)

SUCCESS INDICATORS

What does success look like for you? (e.g. Finding a mentor, securing an internship, building a portfolio)

KEY METRICS

How will you measure your progress? (e.g. Applications submitted, interviews? New reach outs?

CONTINUOUS LEARNING

How will you keep expanding your knowledge and skills?

Sticky Board Part I

Sticky Board Part II

Acknowledgments

This book is dedicated to every student and professional who has ever paused long enough to ask, *"What's next for me?"*

Career clarity is rarely accidental. It is built through reflection, structure, feedback, and the discipline to continually refine direction. Over the years, I've had the privilege of working alongside thousands of individuals navigating that question. Their ambition, uncertainty, resilience, and willingness to engage in the process shaped the thinking behind these pages.

I am especially grateful to the mentors who took me under their wing early in my career—Kimberly Cuff, Denise McCarney, Marianne Rothenberg, Diane Karija, Randy McMills, Gale Rothwell, Vern Kelly, and many others whose names deserve equal recognition. They did more than encourage me; they gave me structure. They challenged assumptions, demanded measurable progress, and held me accountable to standards I had not yet learned to set for myself. They did not simply open doors; they taught me how to evaluate which doors mattered and how to build leverage long before it was required.

Only later did I recognize that they were modeling the very principles this book now teaches: clarity before action, metrics before emotion, preparation before disruption. They accelerated my growth not by removing obstacles, but by equipping me with a framework to navigate them. Their influence lives within every canvas block and decision lens presented here.

To the leaders, colleagues, and hiring teams I have partnered with across decades in Silicon Valley and beyond—thank you for reinforcing that careers are not built on talent alone, but on visibility, disciplined execution, and continuous learning. The *Bullish Career Canvas* was shaped in real conversations, real inflection points, and real decisions that carried weight.

To my family—thank you for your steadiness and perspective. Writing about resilience and growth is easier when surrounded by people who embody both.

And to you, the reader: thank you for choosing intention over drift. Whether you are just beginning or recalibrating mid-journey, I hope this book becomes something you return to—not because you are uncertain, but because you are deliberate.

Careers do not evolve by accident. They evolve when someone decides to design them.

My hope is that the structure and system shared here give you more than guidance—that they give you confidence. Confidence to think strategically. Confidence to measure progress. Confidence to adapt before disruption forces you to.

The work is now yours.

Onward.

.

About the Author

Edward Avila is a Talent Acquisition Executive with more than three decades of experience in Silicon Valley, helping both startups and global corporations build high-performing teams. His career spans semiconductors, high-tech, and AI/data-driven companies, where he has designed recruiting infrastructures, scaled organizations, and partnered with executives to shape the future of work.

Edward is a multi-book author and talent strategist. His earlier titles—*Be Bullish 101: Make the Big Leap from College to the Workplace* and *Be Bullish Zero to Three: What No One Tells You About Your First Three Years at Work*—equip emerging professionals with the structure and insight needed to launch strong careers.

In *Be Bullish The Luminous Path: Build Career Clarity*, Edward expands his focus beyond early-stage talent and introduces the *Bullish Career Canvas*—a 12-block decision framework designed to help students and professionals at any stage build direction, close gaps, and position themselves with intention in an evolving workforce.

Edward holds a Master's in Organizational Development from the *University of San Francisco* and a Bachelor's in Political Science from Loyola Marymount University.

www.ingramcontent.com/pod-product-compliance
Lightning Source LLC
Chambersburg PA
CBHW041310120726
48005CB00014B/1951